Rose's Story

Volume II

Rose Weds in Barbados

Carla M. Cuffee

Copyright © 2020 Carla M. Cuffee

All rights reserved. No part(s) of this book may be reproduced, distributed or transmitted in any form, or by any means, or stored in a database or retrieval systems without prior expressed written permission of the author of this book.

ISBN: 978-1-5356-1740-6

Dedication

I want to create a legacy by becoming an author for my two daughters and their children and their children's children.

Contents

Dedication iii
Prologue 1
Chapter 1: Crane Beach, Barbados 3
Chapter 2: Jotting It All Down 6
Chapter 3: The Office of Diamonds Event Center 9
Chapter 4: Planning Mode 12
Chapter 5: Shopping for a Dress 14
Chapter 6: Dinners at Rose's 17
Chapter 7: One More Dress 21
Chapter 8: DJ Spinn 24
Chapter 9: Four Dresses 26
Chapter 10: Big Eaze's Attire 29
Chapter 11: The Investments 33
Chapter 12: The Wedding Details 39
Chapter 13: Seamstress 44
Chapter 14: Opening up Shop 49
Chapter 15: Planning a Wedding 53
Chapter 16: Measurements 58
Chapter 17: A Second Fitting 64
Chapter 18: A Lot Going On 68
Chapter 19: Rehearsal Dinner 72
Chapter 20: Opening up a Restaurant 75
Chapter 21: Party into the A.M. 82
Chapter 22: Beach Party in Barbados 87
Chapter 23: The Week Goes by Fast 93
Chapter 24: The Key: R&R 99
Chapter 25: Rose's Wedding Day Has Finally Arrived 105
Chapter 26: A Romantic Beach Wedding 110
Chapter 27: Nights like This 115

Prologue

ROSE AND BIG EAZE, AKA Frank, had been traveling the globe. In the blink of an eye, a year and some months had gone by. While traveling, Rose spent a lot of time thinking about setting a date for her and Big Eaze's wedding. While on a business trip in Barbados, she believed the time had finally come around to settle down and plan her wedding. Rose loved the Barbadian sunrises and sunsets, so she thought it would be fitting for her to have a simple yet elegant sunset wedding on Crane Beach in Barbados.

Chapter 1

Crane Beach, Barbados

Rose and Big Eaze had flown out to Barbados on many occasions for business trips, and while there, they'd walked the beach at night, enjoying the laid-back atmosphere, the smell of the ocean water, and the sound of the crashing waves.

One night, while standing on the deck of their villa and looking out onto the deep ocean waters, Rose turned to Big Eaze and said, "I think I would love to have our wedding here. I would love to have it in the evening, right here on the beach, right in front of the ocean. I want to see the perfect sunset drifting off into the moonlit sky, while Caribbean music is played on those steel drums. I can see our families on the beach, laughing and talking and running around between the tiki lights. We'll serve fresh seafood. O-M-G! I can see it." While continuing to look at Big Eaze, she added, "I would love to have a casual yet elegant wedding. We'll have a party of about fifty. We will invite some of our closest friends, along with our families. We'll sit under a canopy that's wrapped in palm trees blowing in the night beach breeze…" Rose was being very animated. "Are you imagining it?" she asked Big Eaze.

"Ah, wait. We'll be sitting on the sand?" Big Eaze asked.

"Of course not, silly. I wasn't finished with the setup. There will be oversized plush pillows for each guest to sit on."

The idea of sitting on oversized pillows on sand didn't sit well with Big Eaze, but when it came to Rose, he would agree to everything that she said when it came to planning events.

So, he said, "I don't see your vision, but that's not my field of expertise. If this is what you want, so be it. But fifty guests? Rose, that alone is the staff, and do you have a date in mind?"

While bobbing her head at Big Eaze, Rose just smirked and said, "Let me handle the wedding details please. You just show up."

A while later, they started their usual walk along the shoreline and listened to the crashing waves as they journeyed. Rose stopped to listen to the waves and said, "Listen … listen to that … ah, that sound." She paused for a moment. "I could never get tired of that sound. It's so calming to the soul."

While standing near the edge of the water, Rose dug her toes into the sand. She turned to look up at Big Eaze and said, "We should set up our lounge chairs on the deck, light a fire in the fire pit, and rest under the night sky. It's full of stars. We can have a glass of wine, turn on some soft Caribbean music." Rose swayed her shoulders. "I'm sure we'll sleep like babies tonight."

"Yeah," Big Eaze said, while walking back to their villa, "that sounds romantic."

They both stopped before approaching their villa to take in the view of the moonlit sky and breathe in the night breeze coming off the ocean water.

Big Eaze turned to Rose, wrapped his arms around her waist, and planted a kiss on her forehead. They stood there for the next ten minutes in total silence before walking back to their villa. While approaching the villa, Big Eaze said, "I'm getting the chairs out right now."

Rose watched while Big Eaze set a fire. After he completed this task, he brought out a blanket to wrap around themselves. They spent the rest of the evening nestled together on their double-sided lounge chair and listened to Caribbean music.

"This is the perfect ending to a long day, sitting on the villa deck, listening to the waves crashing, having a cold glass of Villa Rose Moscato wine … it's like music to my ears. I have to say that this wine is pretty good once it's chilled," said Rose. After a short pause, Rose continued to talk about the details of the wedding. "We should serve the food on the beach under a huge, white linen tent. The tent would need to withstand the breeze that may come off the ocean. It can get a bit breezy out here at night."

While wrapping the blanket tighter around her body, Rose noticed that Big Eaze had not said a word while sitting on their lounge chair. She peeked over and saw that he was fast asleep. *Oh, yeah, very romantic,* thought Rose.

Chapter 2

Jotting It All Down

On the flight back home, Rose was in planning mode. She got out her trusty iPad but wished she had one of her journals, which she had been writing in for years. She had filled several journals with plans for events. Her journals were filled with handwritten notes. She was trying to type some ideas on a beach-themed wedding when they hit more turbulence than she could tolerate. She shut down the iPad and closed her rose-colored, rimmed-in-crystals iPad case. She then closed her eyes and envisioned a beach wedding.

The bride will wear a long, soft white, chiffon gown that easily flows with the wind. The gown will not need much detail, thought Rose, but I would like for the gown to have a V-neckline. Rose smiled as she envisioned her gown. I don't believe much jewelry will be needed; it is a beach wedding. But I will wear some of those beach sandals. I would love for my hair to be pinned in a bun with white pearls wrapped around the bun, she thought. For my Jewels, they can also wear white with their hair pinned up, and they should wear small studded earrings. A simple bracelet would look nice, and there should be no need for a necklace. And we should all, also, wear those beach sandals. For the color theme throughout the wedding party setup, I think I would like the colors, blue, beige, and white. Yeah … I think those colors go well on a beach. And for the groom… umm … I think he would really look nice in a white linen pants set. I don't think he should have on any shoes. But I'll allow him to wear his button-down shirt with a few buttons undone, and I would like for him to wear a gold necklace to show off his cocoa skin, and he could wear a gold bracelet to set off the Caribbean look.

The canopy would need to be wrapped in clear fairy dust lights and trimmed with palm tree branches, which will seat close to fifty guests, nestled on huge pillows.

Rose, still in deep thought, tried to envision the fluffy pillows. Those pillows would need to be huge and so fluffy that a baby could sleep on them. She continued to be so deep in thought, visualizing her beach wedding, that she didn't hear the captain speak into the intercom. He informed the passengers and the crew that they would be at their destination within fifteen minutes, so they would need to return to their seats, put their tray tables up, and buckle their seat belts in order to prepare for landing.

After the announcement, Rose opened her eyes and told Big Eaze that she had the wedding all planned out, but she would still need to find a DJ who would be available for their wedding.

"I want Caribbean music to be played." She looked at Big Eaze for an answer. "Do you have a DJ in mind who would be the best fit for our wedding?" asked Rose. Rose loved to be in control of every detail of her events, so the DJ would need to suit her liking.

Big Eaze said, "I'll let DJ Spinn handle that. He's the manager of six DJs, that he handpicked himself, so he would know."

"Great. I'll call the girls as soon as I get home and let them know we're planning to get married on June first."

"What?" Big Eaze exclaimed. "Thanks for adding me to your plans, but we have the ribbon-cutting ceremony for the opening of the new restaurant on June first. Don't you remember? Look that up in your books." Big Eaze pointed at her iPad case, thinking it was one of her journals.

While holding her iPad close to her chest, Rose gave Big Eaze a hard stare as she said, "This is not for Big E's Enterprises."

"Well, it shouldn't be for A Dozen Roses either. Why are you planning this? We, we ..." Big Eaze, who was exasperated, stuttered, so he paused for a moment. Then, he said, "Your daughters run an event-planning company."

With clenched teeth, Rose said, "Because I want to and because I can!"

Big Eaze turned away from Rose and shook his head while mumbling under his breath. Then, he turned back toward her and said, "Why do you feel the need to plan the wedding? What about Diamonds?"

After asking these questions, Big Eaze expected an answer from Rose, but he got no response from her. They sat quietly for the remainder of the flight.

Chapter 3

The Office of Diamonds Event Center

AFTER SPEAKING WITH SCARLET AND Ruby, Rose made her way over to Diamonds. She did not mention to Scarlet and Ruby, also known as the Divas, that she would be en route to their office. Rose opened the door to her Range Rover, and Chase, their driver, looked back at Rose and asked, "Will we be waiting for Frank?"

"Ha! No way," said Rose. "He has no business where I'm going." She instructed Chase to drive her to the office of Diamonds Event Center, on 10 Foxwood Lane.

When they arrived at Diamonds, Rose let Chase know that she would be there for a while and that she would call him when she was ready to be picked up. Rose let herself out before Chase could open the front door of the Range Rover. Then, she walked into Diamonds.

The front door was open, but no one was sitting out in the reception area to greet Rose, so she banged on the bell and yelled, "Hello! Hello! Anyone here?" She pounded on the front desk bell again and again.

Scarlet, Ruby, and Bridgette were in the back, in the event room, where all the magic and planning happened. Scarlet and Ruby came out to see Rose standing in their place of business. They were pretty much surprised to see her.

"Oh, my! I don't think we've ever seen you here," said Scarlet. "To what do we owe the pleasure of your presence?"

"Yeah," said Ruby. "Normally, we have scheduled meetings for our clients. Are you a client?"

Rose just smirked and lifted her head up. Then, she said that she had a wedding date in mind and that it would be a destination wedding in Barbados. The Divas looked at each other in disbelief, as Scarlet shrieked, "What? We have beautiful beaches here!"

"And ... I want the beautiful beaches of Barbados," said Rose. "There's something about those scenic beaches that attract me."

"Well, a girl knows what she wants," said Ruby. "So why are you here? Are you hiring our services to plan your wedding?"

"Yes and no. I would like for you girls to help me plan the wedding," said Rose.

"No way, Mom. You have an event-planning company that you passed down. Why are you planning the wedding? You don't trust that we know how to plan a lavish wedding? Or do you not think we know how to take instructions from you?" asked Scarlet.

"See. There it is. Why does everything have to be lavish? Why can't it be simple, elegant, and pure?" Rose said, and Scarlet just stared at her. "So now that I have your attention. I have all I want right here," and she showed the Divas the iPad, which was still in its case.

"O-M-G! She done brought the books out again. What? Are you not busy enough?" asked Scarlet.

"Come on! Let Mom plan her wedding the way she wants to plan it. It is her wedding, and we have no right to dictate to her what she wants. That's why it's called event planning ... it's planned," Ruby said with a giggle.

Rose just smiled and walked toward the event room, where all the magic and planning happened, which was located in the back of the building.

Chapter 4

Planning Mode

Rose described what type of dress she wanted to wear to the Divas, as well as what she wanted for them to wear. Then, she described what Big Eaze would wear because she could not forget about the groom. While discussing the wedding apparel and where the wedding would be held, the Divas slowly came around to the idea of a destination wedding.

As Rose was describing the dimensions of the canopy and what it should look like, Ruby pulled out her laptop and digitally created the canopy. Then, she showed them her design.

Rose was shocked but very pleased and excited that Ruby had gotten the design as perfect as she did. It was like seeing it in person.

"Well done, Ruby," Rose said enthusiastically. "That was fast and so on point. So on to the next phase then. I would love large plush pillows under the canopy. I was thinking of the colors of beige, white, and blue. But now, after thinking it over, I would I like to see blue with white stripes, like in a blue jean material, you know, to give it a nautical feel."

Scarlet asked, "How many guests will you have?"

"Close to fifty of our closest friends and family," Rose answered.

Scarlet, looking a bit puzzled, asked, "So we'll have fifty pillows under a canopy?"

"Okay, okay. If we use the villa, it would be kind of tight, like everyone is sitting right on top of us while we recite our wedding vows. We can build temporary seating," Rose said, sounding a little annoyed.

"I have a couple more questions," Scarlet said. "The reception, would that also be on the beach? And have you thought about all of your friends that would love to see you get married? I mean, they were there at your birthday ball, and they witnessed Big Eaze propose to you."

"Yeah, but I want a small, intimate wedding. I'm in my fifties and have no need for a large, formal wedding."

"Okay. You know what you want, but I'm sure you'll have some explaining to do later," said Scarlet. She was not at all happy with her mom's decision to have a small wedding. She thought that Rose's friends would have loved to be at her and Big Eaze's wedding.

After a long silence, Bridgette decided to break it. She asked, "How about having a formal reception when you come back home?"

All three women looked at Rose for a response.

"I don't see why not. Let's stick with white linen and create a tropical theme in the garden." She smiled at Bridgette for coming up with that idea and said, "Thanks."

"You're welcome," said Bridgette. She was so excited that she was able to come up with an idea that pleased Rose. She was new at Diamonds and wanted to make a good impression on Rose and the Divas.

Chapter 5

Shopping for a Dress

Rose continued to look for the prefect dresses for her jewels and herself. She had looked in countless wedding magazines and on many websites for a dress that would catch her eye. She'd become pretty agitated and frustrated with the gown search.

As she threw up her hands, just about ready to give up, Bubbles, who was headed to the outside pool, walked by her office, popped her head in, and said, "Hi, G'ma. What you doing?"

Rose was startled by Bubbles's sudden appearance, but after regaining her composure, she explained her ordeal to her granddaughter, "I'm having a horrible time finding the perfect dress."

Bubbles stepped back and said, "I can create one for you. What kind of dress do you have in mind"?

"Huh! You can create what? Okay. I'm done here," Rose exclaimed and shut the computer down. While walking toward Bubbles, who was eleven years old, Rose said, "If you can create a dress, I'll … I'll … I don't know what I'll do." She walked past Bubbles, shaking her head in disbelief.

What Rose didn't know was that Bubbles had been creating clothing designs on a daily basis.

***

Later that day, after returning from shopping, Rose walked through the front entrance with an armful of what appeared to be wedding gowns. As she approached Evelyn, Rose was smiling from ear to ear. She asked Evelyn to assist her with the gowns by helping her carry them to her walk-in closet.

Evelyn summoned up more staff to assist with all the gowns that were in Rose's truck. Chase, her driver, pointed them out. One staff person returned with a clothing rack to hang the gowns on because Rose had picked up about twenty gowns, all in different shades, shapes, and lengths. They hurried to her closet, rolling the gowns along with them.

Rose put on the first gown. Then, she spun around to face Evelyn and said, "I'll need to try on all of these gowns to see which one I like the best. Better yet, after I find the one that looks fabulous on me and looks great with my skin tone, I will donate the ones that I don't want." She paused while Evelyn assisted her with zipping up the first gown.

***

After an hour of trying on gowns, Rose seemed pleased with the handful that she'd put on a separate clothing rack to show her Jewels when they came over for dinner on Sunday. While still assisting Rose, Evelyn said, "You have picked out some really good ones, but you can only wear one. You have a tough decision to make, Rose."

Looking at what was left on the dress rack, Rose said, "You're

Rose's Story

absolutely right, Evelyn," so she went through them again and again and continued to pick out what she felt wasn't appealing enough to keep. After the last round of elimination, while looking at the rack, Rose said, "Okay. I have narrowed it down to seven. Is this better?"

"Well, you can only wear one, but this is a start," said Evelyn.

Chapter 6

Dinners at Rose's

"Wow! This is different for you, Rose. Pizza and wings? We normally have a full-course meal, like meat, veggies, and some sort of starch."

This wedding planning must be getting to her because this is so not like Rose, thought Ruby.

Scarlet came in from the outside garden, yelling that she should have brought Rose a pizza oven. "That was my first thought for a birthday gift," she yelled.

"All right. I would like to change it up a little today, so after we eat, I would like to have a bridal fashion show," Rose said.

Bubbles perked up when she heard the words "fashion show." While in her room, she had designed a gown that she wanted to share with her G'ma. Excitedly, she thought, this is the perfect time to show off my design. But Bubbles was feeling a little nervous and unsure if they would take her seriously. Heck! Lately, she was not really sure what was going on with all the drawings.

The pizza and wings were served in the outside garden. There were

Rose's Story

about ten boxes of pizza for the family and staff, and there was a variety to choose from — steak with onion and peppers, bacon and pepperoni, spinach with sliced tomatoes that came with a white sauce, spinach and garlic chicken, seafood (which was one of Rose's favorite), Hawaiian with banana peppers, of course, the traditional pepperoni and sausage, and cheese.

Rose had also ordered six pans of wings in six different flavors, which included traditional buffalo sauce, a Cajun-style dry-rub, garlic parmesan, barbecue sauce, spicy honey glazed, and wings wrapped in brown sugar bacon. Wow! Finger-licking good!

The temperature that evening was about 75 degrees. Rose had the garden setup so beautifully. With flowers of every color, a nice-sized gazebo that sat next to a small pond and feet away from a rock garden and a nice-sized pool, it was a vision to behold.

The pool had a well-lit under path, so when anyone swam out of the under path, they were led to a private, secluded rainfall. The only sounds that could be heard were the thundering of water splashing against the mountain rock walls.

The garden also housed a massive waterfall wall. It was made of stone, which also was used as a movie screen for outdoor movie nights.

Soft music played as the water flowed at a gentle pace, hitting the rocks, seeming to create its own tunes and a piece of art. The art like view showed a backsplash of blue lights hitting against the stone wall.

There were plentiful lights throughout the garden, which glowed softly against a well-kept green lush lawn. It had tall and thick hedges, shaped to perfection, which provided extra privacy for the garden.

The guests sat in anticipation of the first model. Everyone thought Evelyn and her staff would be strutting down the catwalk, so they were all surprised when they saw Rose walking down the well-lit garden path.

As Rose modeled the first gown, everyone could see that there was a train on the gown, and as she walked, the garden lights showed her gown rippling against the cemented path. She stopped in front of her family, turned to face them, and saw that they all looked very surprised.

Scarlet yelled out, "Wait! You're not supposed to let Big Eaze see you in your wedding gown."

"Awe ... that's so traditional, and I'm not a traditional kind of girl," said Rose.

Following that first dress, Rose modeled all seven of her gowns, and each one was very different. Rose wanted everyone's opinion on each of the gowns. After she had modeled all the gowns, she instructed her family and staff to locate the pieces of paper and pens that were at each table. She, then, asked each one of them to give an opinion on each gown, as to how she fit the gown and how it looked while she walked in it. The other questions were, was the color appealing? Was it the right shade? Was it too slimming? Too puffy? Too short? Too long? Rose gave instructions as she walked away, looking amazing.

It was late by the time everyone had completed their votes and had handed them in. They had been instructed to give their pieces of paper to Evelyn, who placed them in a glass jar.

After everything had been collected, Rose thanked them all for taking time out to participate in her bridal show and for giving her feedback on each gown. She invited all who wanted, both staff and family, to take what was left of the pizzas and wings. Before leaving, the staff was asked to return the garden to its previous state.

Rose's Story

    Bubbles was the last to leave the garden. She was so nervous that she did not want to interfere with the bridal show, so she waited for another time.

Chapter 7

One More Dress

BUBBLES WAS HANGING WITH HER G'ma on a beautiful sunny afternoon. Rose said, "No more baking cookies here. We're going to get baked cookies and have some tea."

"Sounds nice, G'ma. Do you still go to Karma's Bakery Shop, or have you found a new spot?" asked Bubbles.

"Well, we can find another spot if you'd like, but I just love the cookies that they have at Karma's. They're soft. They're gooey and, sometimes, sticky. They come in the right size, not too big and not too small, and when you walk in the place, you just about want to buy all that she has baked for the day. But you know I have to watch of my figure." Rose laughed at her comment. "I am getting married."

"Yeah, on a beach," said Bubbles.

"In Barbados." Rose smiled from ear-to-ear while shaking her head.

Rose noticed Bubbles's sketchbook. She was curious about it, so she asked, "What is that book about? I've noticed that you carry it everywhere you go?"

To Bubbles's surprise, she looked down and noticed that she had her sketchbook attached to a latch, tucked under her arm. She had become so attached to it that she often forgot she was even carrying it at times. "Yes, it's my new clothing accessory," she said.

They both laughed at Bubbles's comment as they were getting into Rose's Range Rover.

Karma's was not a very big place, but it had enough parking space next to the shop. They walked into the shop, and the aroma of sweet baked cookies hit them hard. As they approach the counter and greeted by the cashier, Rose asked for her favorite dozen of cookies and a glass of cold tropical berry tea. "I don't like it hot," she said as she looked at her granddaughter.

Bubbles ordered a dozen of her favorite dark chocolate cookies and a cup of regular hot tea. She instructed the cashier to make her tea very hot and to add two scoops of sugar. She also asked the cashier for a spoon.

Again, Karma's was not a very big place, but it was big enough to have about ten tables. Rose and Bubbles were able to find a booth next to a window. They sat and chatted and laughed 'til their tummies hurt. This was their special time together. Rose tried to set a time aside in her busy schedule, so she could spend time with her granddaughter. She strived to have monthly outings with her.

Bubbles was feeling a lot more comfortable now that she had her G'ma alone and was not facing a host of people. She opened up her sketchbook and turned the page to where she'd sketched a gown that she wanted to share with her. Bubbles was a little hesitant, but she really wanted to share her design with Rose.

"G'ma, I know you were feeling really good about the gowns that you modeled at your fashion show last Sunday, and I'm not sure if this is what you're looking for, but I wanted to show you what I designed for you."

The gown that Bubbles had designed was a white gown that seemed to be very flowy. Bubbles had placed embroidered lace at the top of the gown, and she had drawn a V-neckline because she thought that her G'ma would be comfortable in an open neckline. The bottom of the dress was chiffon, and she had made it a very long dress. It appeared that the gown would drag in the sand. It was an elegant and gorgeous gown. It seemed to be very comfortable, even on a sandy beach.

Rose's eyes shone like diamonds as she looked at her granddaughter's design. She was floored. With her hand over her mouth and the other on her chest, she teared up and said, "This is perfect. This is exactly what I had envisioned. I love it. Did you draw this?"

"Yes, I've been designing for a while now. What do you think?" asked Bubbles.

"What do I think?" said Rose, who was still in shock. She finally asked Bubbles, who was no more than eleven years old. "Are you able to design your mom, your aunty, and yourself a dress? If this is asking too much, I understand. Do you even know how to sew? If not, it's not a problem. I can take the designs to a seamstress to have them made." Again, Rose was still in shock, so she asked Bubbles, "Would you like for your name to be on a label? Do you even have a label?"

"I don't know. I'm just starting this," said Bubbles.

Rose sat back. She was still in shock, but she was very happy that she had found her perfect gown, fit for an evening beach wedding in Barbados.

Chapter 8

DJ Spinn

Big Eaze had spoken with DJ Spinn, regarding the wedding, and had asked him to book a DJ who could travel to the Caribbean. DJ Spinn called Rose because he wanted to meet with her.

"Sure. How about lunch today in the garden?" said Rose.

"Would two o'clock be too late for lunch?" asked DJ Spinn.

"Aww. Yeah. That would be a late lunch, but if that's the time you have, so be it. I'll see you then."

***

DJ Spinn arrived on time and was escorted to the garden. Rose was sitting at the table when DJ Spinn was seated.

"Have you eaten at all today?" asked Rose.

"Yes, something small, about eleven this morning. I have to get it in when I can. We run a tight schedule," DJ Spinn said.

"Yeah. Are you planning on hiring more DJs?"

"I would like to. I'm looking into writing up a proposal for Big Eaze. I'm thinking we need an additional four DJs. Two would be part-time, for young children's and teenagers' parties, and I would like for the other two to rap, you know, get the crowd pumped, talk, and dance with the people, you know, not just play music."

Rose chuckled. "That sounds like an aerobics class to me, but a great plan, Spinn. Write it up, so we can move on it right away."

"Thanks. So down to the business at hand. I, myself," he said, while pointing at himself, "would love to host the music for your wedding. It would be an honor for me to do this for you and Big Eaze."

"How sweet of you, Spinn, and I'm glad that you asked. I would love to have you host the music. Thank you so much, Spinn, and it's an honor to have you on our team, but you do know that it's a destination wedding in Barbados, so I would love to have island music played. I'm not sure if Big Eaze has mentioned this to you, but I would love to hear those steel drums that Caribbean music is played on." She looked at DJ Spinn for approval.

"Yes, that would be appropriate for a beach wedding in Barbados. I'll make it work," said DJ Spinn.

And just that quick, the meeting was over, but DJ Spinn stayed a little while longer, chatting about upcoming events and how thin the staff was at the time being. He mentioned that he had to fill in sometimes, which was keeping him away from scouting out other DJs to come on board.

While finishing a tall glass of iced tropical berry tea. DJ Spinn mentioned that he would write up the proposal that evening and forward it over to Big E's Enterprises' office inbox. Then, he kissed Rose's hand and left the garden.

Chapter 9

Four Dresses

Bubbles and Rose had been spending a lot of time together. Bubbles had been hard at work, designing the dresses. She was in constant contact with Rose. At the moment, Rose was waiting for Bubbles outside her after-school program at school. As Bubbles emerged from the building, she saw her G'ma waiting in her Range Rover, which was easy to spot because she was parked right in front of the building.

Bubbles sighed when she approached the truck and said, "Wow, G'ma! We've been spending way too much time together."

"Well, hello to you, too," said Rose. "Get in. I just want to see your progress on the dresses. How about it? What's the progress on them?" asked Rose, while Bubbles was getting in the back seat of the truck.

"Just finishing up," Bubbles said. "I do have a life outside of this. I have school. I attend an after-school program … uh … homework, my friends, my mom."

"Well, be expecting this when you get older and your job looks for perfection. They'll be looking over your shoulder, monitoring every move you make," said Rose with a laugh.

"And I'll work for my mom," said Bubbles as she closed the truck door.

Then, Rose looked in her rearview mirror and drove off.

"Are you hungry?" she asked her granddaughter.

"No, I had a snack already, and the designs are done," said Bubbles. She pulled her sketchbook out of her book bag and tossed it onto the front seat and sat back, looking out the window, wanting to get back to her life. While looking out the window, Bubbles thought, I never knew this would be so demanding. I can't even enjoy my youth, she thought, just before she drifted off to sleep.

When they arrived at Bubbles's home, Rose woke her granddaughter up. Once she was fully awake, Bubbles realized she was at her home and not at her G'ma's.

"What happened, G'ma? You didn't like the sketches?"

"I haven't seen them yet," said Rose. "I just wanted to bring you home. I'll come in and view the sketches and let you know if they're a go."

"Oh, okay," said Bubbles. "I hope I didn't hurt your feelings, G'ma. I'm just feeling the pressure of an adult life, and I'm just eleven years old."

"Not a problem, my love bug, but at least, you've been able to see what an adult life is like. Responsibility can be a pressure cooker," said Rose.

Ruby was in the kitchen, preparing meatloaf, which was one of Rose's favorite dishes, when she looked up and saw Rose and Bubbles approaching the kitchen.

"Hey, you two! I was expecting Bubbles, but it's a surprise to see you here, Mom. Do you want to stay for dinner?" asked Ruby.

Rose's Story

"Yeah…I smell meatloaf, which is one of my favorites." Rose took a seat in the corner nook. She opened the sketchbook and saw her dress, which she had previously seen. She turned the next page to see another spectacular-looking gown. The gown was designed with a one-shoulder strap, and it was turquoise, which was the color of the Caribbean sea.

Rose smiled. She seemed to be very excited by the choice of color. She continued to turn the page to see another dress. This dress was smaller, but it was the same color as the previous dress and it had two straps. Each dress had the same chiffon bottom as Rose's dress. Rose looked up to see Ruby and Bubbles staring at her, waiting for approval. Rose gave the two thumbs up!

They sat and ate dinner while discussing Bubbles and her dress designs. Rose said that she really thought that Bubbles would be the next in-demand child designer. She said, "Just keep designing. You never know what will come out of this."

Bubbles sat there, smiling, and said, "You're right. You never know!"

Chapter 10

Big Eaze's Attire

Rose did not ask Bubbles to design a white linen suit for Big Eaze because she already had one in mind. She called down to the men's shop that Big Eaze shopped at and spoke with Mitch, Big Eaze's personal clothing expert, and ordered a white linen suit that she'd seen on display.

Rose thought, Big Eaze is always easy to dress. After feeling the pressure of getting her dress and her Jewels dresses picked out, Rose was feeling some sort of relief. She told Mitch to have the suit delivered to the Crystal Manor.

Now that we have the attire picked out, it's time to get the food and the villa setup for an elegant evening wedding on a Barbadian beach, thought Rose. She did not want any glitches to set off, so she wanted to get her books out and get started on the menu and have the villa décor ready in plenty of time.

As she went to get her books, she ran into Big Eaze, who was looking a bit puzzled, and Rose was looking at Big Eaze and wondering, what could be the problem? So, she asked, "Frank, are you

Rose's Story

okay? You're looking a bit puzzled."

Big Eaze turned in Rose's direction and said, "Something is not right with the new investment deal. You know, the new clients coming on board in June? We need to fly out to California right away. We were scheduled to have conference calls every other week, but I have not heard from them in about two weeks. Actually, it's going on three weeks now."

"Don't worry. I'll pack us a bag. How long do you think we'll be there? I am still getting the wedding together. Do you think I should change the date of the wedding? Do you think that I should change the location of the wedding?" Rose asked Big Eaze.

Big Eaze looked at Rose and said, "What's with all the questions? You're handling it, like you handle everything else. Now you want my opinion?"

Rose stayed calm as she thought, we've been down this road before. While walking away, Rose turned to face Big Eaze and said, "You are absolutely correct. Why am I asking you?"

Rose didn't want to cause a rift between them because she knew that weddings seemed to bring out hostility in people. It was a stressful time, which should have been a wonderful time of bonding. I'm no Bridezilla, thought Rose.

Rose called Evelyn to help her pack for her two-day trip. While they were packing, Evelyn asked, "If you don't mind me asking, where are you going now? You should be planning your wedding."

"I can plan while I'm away. I just need to find my books. Have you seen them? I didn't put them away yet, right?" asked Rose.

"Yes, you have. You had me put them in storage six months after you handed the business to Scarlet and Ruby," Evelyn said.

"Just great. More stress. I need them," said Rose, "and I'm going away, so what am I going to write on now? A notebook?" said Rose while rolling her eyes.

"Well, when are you leaving? I can either call for them or go and get you a notebook," said Evelyn.

Rose started to laugh, and Evelyn joined her, not knowing why she was laughing.

"A notebook? I have not used a notebook since I was in high school. I should get it just for the heck of it," Rose said sarcastically. "Better yet, maybe I should see if Bubbles has an extra one." She continued to laugh at herself. "Yeah, that's what I'll do because I don't think I will have time to wait for my books to be delivered," Rose yelled after taking deep breaths.

After getting a kick out of her writing in a notebook, she said, "I really needed that laugh, but please have John come and get the bags. I think we are leaving out soon, and have Chase go and get me a notebook from the pharmacy down the road. Any one will do," said Rose.

Rose watched Evelyn leave the room. She, then, buried her face in the palm of her hands and thought, *Calm down, Rose. Things will turn out just the way they should, but you've got to keep your cool.* Rose knew the stress of handling events and the pressures of working long hours all too well. That was a lot of work, especially in the beginning, but in time, it got easier. *Maybe I should have let my Jewels handle this,* she thought. *Maybe I should stay out of the game now. I am retired.*

Rose, still in deep thought, decided she needed her Jewels to take over and handle the wedding details. Rose, thinking out loud, said,

Rose's Story

"I'm in no mood for these up and down emotions." She paused and pointed in the air. "But I can handle the yeses and nos."

So, she called the Divas and gave them full access to planning the wedding in Barbados.

Chapter 11

The Investments

ROSE, SAM, BIG EAZE, AND four of Big E's Enterprises' investors flew out the very next morning to Santa Monica, California, booked rooms at the Lidos Hotel, which was located in the heart of town.

Big E's Enterprises was opening up a new restaurant in Santa Monica under the name of Lomontes'. The plan was for it to be a high-end restaurant with reasonable pricing.

While retrieving their rooms and making plans for the day, Rose was not in the mood for searching for anyone or sitting in on any meetings, so she agreed to shop, eat, and have a much-needed relaxing spa day.

Rose was sent off to shop while Big Eaze and his investors went in search of the Lomontes' group.

"Well, I won't go alone," Rose said. "Sam will come with me."

Rose was given the black card, and she shooed them away.

Big Eaze had set up a meeting in one of the conference rooms at the Lidos Hotel. Big Eaze and four of his investors had been trying to reach the Lomontes' team for hours. While using the numbers they'd been using for the past year, they came up no longer available or unlisted.

Big Eaze had just about had enough as he looked around the table, pounded his fist hard on the mahogany table, and asked anyone who would dare answer him, if they knew anything or could vouch for this shady group of people.

"You came to me with this deal, and I invested the largest percentage, but I haven't seen anything. What the heck is going on?" After pausing for an answer, Big Eaze continued, "Tell me something or someone better come up with a legit deal because I'm not losing any money in this shadiness."

Each investor seemed to be a bit nervous. They did not want to rat anyone out.

But Rich spoke out and confirmed that he was as alarmed as everyone else who was there.

"We all have money attached to this deal. We have papers with signatures that we can give to the police for them to search for this group," he said.

"Really? Well, it appears to me that we've been catfished," Big Eaze said.

The men's mouths dropped when Big Eaze mentioned being catfished. Big Eaze looked at Rich and said, "Your team came to me, and I asked, 'Have you done any research on this group?' And your answer was 'Yes, we have.'"

"We were shown credentials and a list of other investment deals," said Bob, who was another investor. "What more could we have done?"

"Fly out to meet them, get the addresses of the other investors, show up unannounced, contact the BBB, research their website domain," Big Eaze said, exasperated.

"We have much of that information," Bob said. "We've met with the team. We all met while at a conference. Up to now, they seemed to be legit."

While shaking his head, Big Eaze said, "We have a lot of money tied to this deal. I can't believe that we've been catfished. This is not sitting well with me." The more he thought about it, the more Big Eaze seemed to get more steamed up. "Where is Sam? She needs to get on this right away. I want the police called." While looking around the table, he said, "Did any of you bring anything that shows that we have signed documents for this deal, other than myself?"

All four of the investors had their portfolios out, which showed the credentials of the investment. Next, all they could do was sit and wait for Rose and Sam to return from shopping.

***

In the meantime, Rose and Sam were taking in the sights of Santa Monica. While sipping on champagne, Rose got a fresh coat of nail polish, along with a pedicure. Rose looked over at Sam and asked, "You're not getting your nails done?"

Sam looked at her nails and replied, "I just got them done. I'm good."

Rose stared at Sam for a long moment. Then, she continued to close her eyes while she enjoyed the sweet aroma of essentials oils that were poured into the pedicure bath.

Afterward, they had a fine cuisine lunch at Simon's Seafood Restaurant, which was close to their hotel.

Next, they were set to go out shopping for new handbags, and not long after, Rose bought herself a rose-colored Chanel purse. She looked at Sam and asked, "You're not buying anything?"

"No," Sam said while lifting up her purse and showing off her three-thousand-dollar Fendi purse, "I don't need a new handbag." She frowned each time Rose asked her about purchasing an item.

"Okay," Rose said, bending over to look Sam straight into her eyes. "We did say that we are going on a spa date, so that's next, okay?" Rose looked at Sam for approval.

They hopped in their taxi limo and headed back to the hotel for a much-needed, relaxing, mind-shifting full-body massage.

While every muscle in her body was being massaged and with the sultry smell of vanilla and sandalwood oils in the air, Rose drifted off into a deep sleep.

***

When Rose awoke, it was about three o'clock in the afternoon. She got dressed and headed out to see Sam sitting on the plush, off-white couch, reading a magazine.

Rose asked Sam, "Did you get a massage?"

"Nope. I didn't need one," said Sam. "I do yoga every day."

"Why did you come with me if you didn't need anything?" asked Rose.

"Well, you asked me to tag along, and I'm not exactly sure why we are even here in California. I'm unaware of any changes in my monthly calendar."

"Umm ... let's go. I'm done for the day," said Rose, looking at Sam, utterly disappointed in her for not purchasing anything but also a little puzzled as to why Sam was not aware that Big Eaze had not heard from the Lomontes' team.

They had dinner reservations for seven that evening in the hotel restaurant, and when they arrived back at their rooms, Big Eaze asked to see Sam. He asked Sam to get together all the investors' credentials because he believed that they had been catfished and wanted to be ready for the police or FBI to assist with any research that they came up with.

Sam asked, "Why am I calling the police?"

Big Eaze, in an uproar, said, "Again, we have been catfished! Did you not hear me? There is no Lomontes'. We have been trying to reach them for hours, to no avail. We have not been able to get in contact with either member with the numbers that we have."

Sam, who was a bit puzzled, went to retrieve the numbers that were given to her from the Lomontes' group to see if they matched up with what Big Eaze had.

After Sam viewed both lists, she told Big Eaze that they were not the same numbers.

"What!" yelled Big Eaze. "When were you going to tell me this? I have been waiting for a conference call for three weeks and have been ready to end this deal because we have not received a call."

Now Sam seem to be getting upset because of a shift in their calendar. She raised her voice as she said, "Because they are out of the country! They are attending a wedding. Now tell me this. Why would I have given you the numbers? I am the one that created the schedules and set up the meetings and the conference calls, and yes, I am the one that patches you into all the calls." She ended by pointing at herself.

"What?" yelled Big Eaze as he pulled up the schedule. "I have to see this for myself, and if this is the case, why didn't you say anything when I scheduled a flight to come out here?"

"You got me," Sam said, shaking her head. "I figured that you had other plans that I was unaware of." Then, while speaking slowly, she said, "There have been many times that we are not on the same page, Frank. I have been complaining about that for the past two years. Stop making and cancelling appointments without me knowing. I'm your secretary. You're not mine." Speaking even slower, she continued, "I need to know these things in order to do my job. You are paying me to do a job. You are not giving me a handout. Those days are over. It has been over ten years since my father and I came to you looking for a job. I now have that job. I have worked up to my current position, and it is my job to handle your business affairs."

Big Eaze felt like crawling into his skin. He was looking a bit embarrassed. "Oh, boy! I messed up. I feel like a fool. I only want the very best for best friend's daughter. I promised him that I would take care of you, look after you like you were my child. I feel, I feel like I haven't been listening. Aww! I failed you … I'm so sorry. Please forgive me."

Sam patted him on the shoulder and said, "You're forgiven, but please don't go back to your old ways because I know I've mentioned this to you before."

Rose stood there in disbelief and started to laugh and laugh and laugh. As she did so, Sam, along with Big Eaze, joined in. After the good belly laugh, they went to look for the other investors to let them know that there had been a huge misunderstanding and that Big Eaze was going to reimburse them for their trip.

Big Eaze, Rose, Sam, and the investors had dinner, took in a Broadway show, headed off to bed, and were back home the very next day.

Chapter 12

The Wedding Details

The Divas went straight to work because they had close to five months before the wedding was to take place. Scarlet went over the beach theme, one more time, to confirm where Rose wanted to wed.

"Are you sure you want to wed at the villa? I'm sure we could find a larger area on the beach where the entire wedding could be hosted because we do need the room," Scarlet said.

"The villa," Rose said. "I think it's best, but I do believe that we need to come up with more seating."

"Okay," Ruby said. "The deck, as you previously mentioned … we can build an oval-shaped seating area, which we can design to fit a little over fifty people. I also was thinking that we can add a temporary deck to set the canopy on, facing the ocean, which the bride and groom, along with the priest, will stand on to recite their vows."

"That sounds great," said Rose. "I'm in favor of that. I also would like to incorporate in the seating area pillows, in the colors of white, and —"

Scarlet politely interrupted Rose before she was done speaking.

"The colors that you previously mentioned are not the colors of an elegant wedding, Mom, and you said that you wanted a small but elegant wedding." As Rose tried to object, Scarlet continued, "Hear me out. I was thinking about incorporating white and adding sheer white to give it a softer feel. Maybe add some gray, sage, and a hint of yellow. What do you think?"

"I like it, and I like it a lot," said Rose, "but I would have those colors in a country wedding, with beautiful flowers and butterflies. Before you interrupted me, I wanted to say that I love the color that Bubbles came up with when designing the three dresses. It's turquoise, the color of the Caribbean sea. How dreamy would that be?"

"Okay," Scarlet said as she added that piece of information to her journal and made a note that the pillows would all be in a soft white.

Scarlet continued to type in her journal: "I think I will add pillows with fringes, which would also give it a beachside feel." She saw the vision of when the wind blew and knew the fringes would also. Scarlet did not share that piece of information; she just added it in her journal.

"Bubbles, did you bring the sketches? I would like to take them to a seamstress on Monday morning," Rose said.

Bubbles tore the pages with designs out of her sketchbook and handed them over to Rose. Rose was making herself a reminder in her phone to call a seamstress on Monday early morning while retrieving the sketches and thanking Bubbles.

"Food?" asked Ruby as she looked in Rose's direction. "Will the catering staff be joining us, or will you be hiring a local Barbadian cratering company for the food service?"

"Well, it would need to be catered there in Barbados. Chef Brew is booked for the full month of June. I do feel more comfortable with our staff, but no one knew that I had the wedding date in mind."

Rose handed over a list of items that she wanted served at the beach wedding. Then, she read over her list out loud, "This is a seaside wedding, so I believe that seafood is fitting for this occasion. With that being said, I'd like to have shrimp cocktail, steamed clams, a smoked salmon dip with bruschetta bread. I'd also like sushi and lobster tails with a lemon sauce. Add large pasta shells stuffed with spinach crab dip … ah … grilled shrimp and vegetable skewers. We can serve a spicy sauce on the side for dipping. Also, king crab legs and large seared scallops wrapped in bacon. I would like to have two types of salmon, one cold and the other baked with sliced lemons and herbs."

"How about a seafood crab salad?" Scarlet suggested. "That also goes well with that bruschetta bread?"

"Sounds good," Rose said. "I would, also, like to have fresh fruit served on a bay of ice and have some of the larger fruits, like watermelon and pineapples, carved into baskets that hold the smaller fruit. You know, like little shapes of fruit, add them to the fruit baskets."

Ruby nodded to acknowledge that she understood. "Okay. I see the vision. Now what else?"

"White wine and iced tea, but make sure that there is a variety of flavored iced teas. Oh, don't forget to add water to the list," said Rose.

It became very quiet.

Scarlet broke that silence when she said, "Okay. Anything else we might have missed?"

"I think we just about covered it. We're staying in the villa. Wait. Now that we are talking about the stay, where will the guests sleep? Your villa only has six rooms," Ruby said. "We would need to know who all will be attending, and I mean, like ASAP, so we can have hotel rooms set aside. I would like to set aside rooms on the Crane Beach Resort. Okay. Let's talk about invitations. I think we have the perfect wedding invitation." Ruby nodded to Bridgette, who went to get it from the showroom.

Bridgette showed Rose an invitation that was white with palm trees as the borders.

"Well, this would be good for the garden party but not for the wedding," Rose said as she examined the invitation.

"Umm…okay. We need to shop for invitations like yesterday," said Ruby, looking at Bridgette, indicating she should add that to the to-do list.

"The invitations will need to mailed out no later than next week. With that, we would need the names of the guests right away," Ruby said while writing in her journal and looking up at Rose.

"You got it, and the music will be hosted by our very own DJ Spinn," said Rose.

"Does he have any experience with island music?" asked Scarlet. "I'm sure that is what you want, right?" She looked at Rose for approval.

"It's all taken care of, and he has asked to do this, so if he asks, then he knows what is expected," Rose said.

"Great. I'm done here," Scarlet said. "We need to get measurements for the additional deck, and I need to order pillows. Do you want to be responsible for the food?" Scarlet asked Ruby.

"No." Ruby chuckled. "I will do the deck. Remember I designed it, and Rose approved it, but I will need to get the wedding invitations together." Ruby stressed that they needed to be mailed out next week. She pushed out her chair and stood up, and Bridgette followed suit.

While walking away, Ruby said, "We should meet again next

Wednesday. Would this day work for everyone, and if so, what time would be best?"

Scarlet said that she would be out of town on a business trip but would send over a text or try to connect via FaceTime. "The best time that I would be able to call in …" Scarlet paused while going through her phone. "Would be about two p.m. that day."

"And I will let you all know where we are with the dressmaking, hopefully, by Tuesday. I'm sure they'll need measurements from us all," said Rose.

Chapter 13

Seamstress

Rose was aware that Evelyn's cousin Carlotta was a seamstress, so she asked Evelyn to reach out to Carlotta and schedule a meeting to discuss employment. Carlotta was currently going to school to become an interior and fashion designer, so she immediately agreed to meet with Rose for potential work.

Carlotta's dream was to open a boutique one day, so she was very interested to see what Rose had in mind for her to do. This will give me a huge push on being a big client of hers, she thought.

They scheduled a Saturday mid-afternoon lunch meeting in the garden.

***

Carlotta arrived fifteen minutes early with a bag filled with seamstress supplies. She wanted to be ready on the spot for any alterations, if needed. She was guided to the garden seating area where she was scheduled to meet with Rose. Carlotta saw Rose approaching from the sliding doors of the guest house with a tray in her hand, and Evelyn followed with a pitcher of tropical berry tea and glasses.

"Hi," Rose said, and Evelyn introduced Rose to her cousin.

Carlotta stood to shake Rose's hand and said, "It's nice to finally meet you in person."

Rose was not sure why she mentioned that. Had Evelyn spoken about her to her family? Rose pretended to have wanted to meet her as well and said, "Likewise."

They were seated at a large table with a huge umbrella to shield them from the raging sun. Rose placed a platter of finger sandwiches on the table and asked Carlotta to have a bite to eat while they got to know each other better. Rose wanted to know a little more about what Carlotta was currently doing and what her plans for the future were, especially regarding her goal to become a seamstress.

Carlotta went on for about fifteen minutes about on her goals and aspirations. She was currently in school full-time and was working part-time as a seamstress for a small cleaner near her home. She had been hanging up and passing out flyers in grocery stores, libraries, and anywhere else where she could get some exposure.

"I network with bridal shops and wedding shows. In the past, I've done some work with major department stores like Lane Bryant, Macy's, and JCPenney, and I also work closely with my family and friends."

She was really trying to get her name out there. She hopefully would open up a boutique where she could sell her designs and manage about five seamstresses or tailors.

"I really love what I do and have a lot of passion for this field," she said while smiling at Rose, hoping to give a good impression of herself as a hard-working woman.

Rose's Story

Rose said, "Wow! You seem to be pretty busy. You've got big goals for yourself. Keep at it and stay focused and be patient. The dream that you have to become a designer will happen."

Rose looked at the bag that Carlotta had brought with her and asked, "Would you happen to have brought any pieces with you or pictures of things that you've created?" asked Rose.

"Yes, I do," Carlotta exclaimed. She was so excited to be showing Rose her work. She pulled a dress out of her bag that she had designed for her niece's middle school homecoming dance.

Rose inspected the dress and said, "Very nice, Carlotta. I really like this piece. You have chosen very good, wrinkle-free material. That was very smart."

"Thank you, Ms. Rose. I really appreciate you saying that. I work really hard, and again, I am very passionate about what I do. I would consider myself a perfectionist."

Rose chuckled. "I know the feeling." She continued to view the dress inside out, carefully observing the neckline and the length of the dress. She looked up at Carlotta and said, "Well, I really like this piece, and I would like to hire you to create four pieces of work that have been already designed. Would you like to work for me on creating these pieces?"

"Yes, I would love that, Ms. Rose ... thank you so much for considering me," Carlotta exclaimed.

"Great! For starters, I need for you to sign a disclosure. Are you okay with that?"

Carlotta looked a bit puzzled. She wasn't sure why she would need to fill out a disclosure. She thought, If Evelyn has worked for Rose for all these years, I'm sure it's okay, so she agreed to sign the disclosure.

After viewing Carlotta's signature and taking the form, Rose continued to mention that she would be getting married in five months and that she had four dresses that her granddaughter had designed. "I really love them," Rose said as she showed Carlotta the designs.

"Very nice," Carlotta said. "Your granddaughter's name is Me'chelle?"

Rose looked at the designs, which was signed by Bubbles using her birth name. She said, "Yes, she will get the credit for the designs, and you will get the credit for sewing them." Rose smiled at the idea that Bubbles had signed her designs and that Carlotta had agreed to sew them. Rose continued to think while nibbling on a finger sandwich, we are finally moving along.

They both continued to chat about the gown designs that Carlotta was to sew. Rose asked Carlotta if she had a place that she created her designs, a working area.

Carlotta said, "No, I currently do not, but I do work out of my family's basement. I have a small section that I call my office. It's very tiny, but it works for now." She looked at Rose.

"Not to worry. If you'd like a bigger place to work out of, I will look for a place for you. I know that it can become a bit cramped when you have to have more than one person over for measurements. Let me get back to you in a couple of days on my findings, okay?" Rose said.

"O-M-G! Thank you so much. That would be much appreciated. More room to create is much needed. I can have more of my things organized, instead of working out of a suitcase, which will make it easier and faster to get things done. Again, Ms. Rose, I thank you for this great opportunity. I won't let you down and hope to be an employee of yours in the future."

Rose's Story

Carlotta wanted to seal the deal by working full-time for Rose, but at the moment, all she could do was smile at Rose, who thanked Carlotta but did not give her a definite answer, regarding working full-time. Carlotta had to prove to Rose that she could get things done one time, and Rose needed to be pleased with her work.

Not wanting to leave Carlotta hanging on the idea of working full-time, Rose said, "Let's just work on these four gowns for now, and we'll see about a position. I'm not really into having things made. I will keep your information and circulate your name throughout my family and friends and my colleagues." Rose shrugged her shoulders, not wanting to give Carlotta false hope.

Carlotta agreed with Rose but was feeling a bit embarrassed for pushing so hard on employment, but she also thought, you have to be aggressive in this field, so she didn't want to linger long on that idea and summed it up as being permissive.

Chapter 14

Opening up Shop

ROSE FOUND A TEMPORARY SPACE for Carlotta to set up her seamstress shop, which was located in a quiet business area. She had set up a six-month deal with the owner of a building that also housed a local pharmacy/old-fashioned ice cream parlor. Rose took Carlotta by the shop and mentioned that she would be able to move into the place the following week to set up and get started creating the gowns.

When the following week finally arrived, Carlotta was in such a good mood while putting her things in place. She was overly excited about where the shop was located, especially because it was near an ice cream parlor. Ah! I will, for sure, get more business being located here, Carlotta thought while she put up shelves to hold garments and bins to house ribbons and threads. She also brought over a very old but trusty sewing machine that was passed down from her grandmother and a newer one that she'd brought a year ago, just in case the old one failed her. This may be a temporary spot for me, but at this moment, it's my space to create, Carlotta thought as she finally saw her dream come to pass. She excitedly spun around and looked at all the items that she had put in place within the past two days. She was hoping to be finished with the four dresses within a couple of weeks. She planned on working long nights and all weekend to get them done, all while going to school full-time. *This is my opportunity, and I'm not going to let it go. It's my time to shine. I want to show the world how serious I am about my craft,* thought Carlotta while starring out of the front window of the store as she watched people walk by and glance into the shop.

Carlotta wanted to use the space after she was done with the dresses for the wedding, which was okayed by Rose. She planned on using the space to create more items for clients that she had picked up after making her niece's dress for the homecoming dance.

While Rose was over one afternoon, Carlotta wanted to pay Rose for the extra months. She asked how much she would need to pay for the space. Rose, not knowing how well Carlotta would do with the extra business, asked, "How many clients and garments can you have set up within these six months, and would you be the only one creating these items?" asked Rose.

Carlotta pulled out her phone and counted the items to be made for her clients' daughters homecoming dance, and she also had pickup other clients requesting her service in creating couture apparel. She said, "Yes, I will be the only person at this time. I do call on my niece from time to time but only with cleanup." Carlotta went on to tell Rose that she had about nine garments to make and felt that they would be done within the six-month time frame.

Rose said, "I really don't like to be in your business regarding your finances, but with the nine items, would that be over a thousand dollars?" she asked Carlotta.

"Yes," Carlotta said, "more like thirty-five hundred dollars, and I hope that I can pull in more before the six months are up."

"I hope you're not overdoing it, seeing as how you are the only one creating these garments" said Rose, while looking at Carlotta strangely.

"Don't worry about me. I am ready for this. I've been waiting a very long time for this great opportunity," Carlotta said while always smiling.

"Okay. Well, with that said, I would like for you to give five-hundred dollars to your local youth center. Write up an invoice and have them sign off on it, so you can account for where you sent your earnings."

***

Within a few days, Carlotta was introduced to Bubbles, who had visited the shop with her G'ma more than once that week, while Carlotta continued to get the shop exactly how she wanted it setup. She was ready to start on the dresses right after she was done setting up her new workspace. She had requested to have Scarlet, Ruby, Bubbles, and Rose over for a full body measurement.

While Rose was at the shop that week, she mentioned that Scarlet was out of town but should be back by Friday. So, Carlotta scheduled all four of them to come over on Friday evening for measurements.

Carlotta wanted to start cutting the garments and the other details on the dresses that weekend. She had Rose look at the white garments that she currently housed in the shop. Rose was not pleased with what Carlotta had shown her and said, "This white will make me look like a marshmallow, and this white looks like fluffy egg white. I'm looking for a soft white, more on the chiffon look, for the bottom half, so my

Rose's Story

dress will flow against the tropical beach breeze."

Well, with that, Rose, Carlotta, and Bubbles went out on a field trip in search of that perfect white. While in search of the perfect white garment, Rose thought, this work is never done, and sighed in disbelief.

Carlotta and Bubbles got to know each other more, while walking around the fabric store and talking about garments and patterns and designs and color threads and the difference in size of the threads. Carlotta had offered to teach Bubbles how to sew, but Bubbles was not at all interested in sewing. "No, thanks," said Bubbles. "I'll stick to what I know best, which is designing. I feel more comfortable with that right now."

Carlotta said, "Okay, but if you ever want to, let me know when you think you're ready."

Chapter 15

Planning a Wedding

Rose, along with Ruby and Scarlet, were to come together within a week with their results.

On Wednesday, their scheduled day and time, Rose and Ruby, along with Ruby's assistant, met at Diamonds, while Scarlet was on Skype (because her iPhone was not fully charged), in order to go over their findings.

Rose informed them that she had hired a seamstress and then said, "We are all scheduled for a full-body measurement on Friday evening. I also have the list of friends that I know will be in Barbados and would love to come to the wedding. I must add that the list has significantly grown." She handed the guest list to Ruby, who showed it to Bridgette.

"Seeing as how the guests will be in town that week, they will already have their hotel rooms," Rose said while everyone was looking at the list.

"How did this all come about?" Scarlet asked. Scarlet's Skype kept going in and out because of a poor connection, so she may have missed most of what Rose had said. The screen kept freezing.

"Just so happens that is the week of a culture festival that goes on in town, so I'm guessing most of them will be there anyway ... that's the only thing I could come up with. Can you please FaceTime us next time?" said Rose.

Scarlet said that she would be in early on Friday and that she had ordered the pillows to sit on the inside deck. All of them were being wrapped in white cloth and lace with white chiffon with fringes, which would look very beachy and would flow against the beach breeze coming off the ocean.

Ruby spoke up and let everyone know that she had a local hardware store in Barbados creating the deck and seating with all that Rose had required to be on it. She said, "They've mentioned that the deck and seating will be done two weeks before the wedding."

"I hope so," said Rose.

"I also have the wedding invitations ready," Ruby said as she showed Rose one of the custom-made wedding invitations that were beautifully crafted in a sandy stone color. The middle was embossed with a rose.

Rose carefully looked over the invitation, inside and out. The inside pictures were lovely. One was of a beautiful, dreamy sunset, which also showed a white sandy beach and waves crashing into the turquoise ocean water. Rose smiled and said, "This is more like it, and it's very beautiful. Was this custom-made?" She was now looking at Ruby.

"Yes, so we need to know right away if you're giving us the green light. If we order them today, we should get them by sometime next week and have the invitations mailed out by the end of that week. It's a week later than I wanted, but we have five months to till wedding, which is still enough time to have the guests RSVP, right?" She looked around the table for approval.

"Yeah, I already mentioned the wedding to the people that will already be down there. I'm sure they'll be looking out for an invitation," Rose confirmed.

"Okay. What about the food?" asked Ruby. "Have you scheduled or found a catering company for that date?" She looked over at Rose.

Rose yelled out, "Oh, my! I've been so busy hiring a seamstress and getting a place for her to work out of that I forgot about that part of the wedding."

Scarlet said to Rose, "You must get someone fast. You have a lot on the menu for that day. Do you even know any catering companies in Barbados that will be available at such a short notice?"

Rose called Chef Brew while they were still in their meeting, but the call went straight to his voice mail. Rose left a message asking him to call back right away.

"I'm sure Chef Brew will recommend one or knows someone that can recommend a good company."

Rose, who was now becoming a bit nervous, seeing how they only had five months, which was really not enough time to get a well-established catering company on board. Events of this nature were booked six months to a year in advance, so she hoped that he could come up with someone worthy of cooking the items, and that their food was well cooked and tasty.

Within fifteen minutes of Rose leaving the voicemail, Chef Brew was calling her back. "Yes, Ms. Rose. How may I help you?" he asked.

Rose, with excitement in her voice, said, "Thanks, Chef Brew, for calling back in such a short time. I'm sure Big Eaze has mentioned that we are planning on getting married in June, and yes, it's short notice, and it's in Barbados, and I know from the monthly calendar that Sam creates that you are booked for the full month of June. So, I am asking, do you have a catering company in Barbados that you highly recommend?"

"Aww, Ms. Rose, you are correct. This is very short notice. Let me check my records and see which company I would highly recommend and, also, check their availability. I will get started on it right away and get back to you within an hour or so," said Chef Brew.

Rose was still nervous while clicking her nails on the wood table but agreed to wait to hear from Chef Brew.

"Well, I'm all done for now," Ruby said. "We're just waiting on a call from Chef Brew. I have to get back to work. I'm meeting some potential clients in a few hours. Call me when you hear back from Chef Brew."

Scarlet also agreed that she was leaving the meeting but also wanted to know what Chef Brew had in store and said that she would call back later that day. Everyone had left the meeting but Rose, who was feeling down about the catering company. She sat there for a moment in deep thought. Then, she called Chase to pick her up at Diamonds.

***

Later in the day, Rose received a call back from Chef Brew with exciting news. He said that he would cater the wedding because he was not able to get a commitment from one of the catering companies that he wanted to highly recommend. He said that he was advised that, in Barbados, they scheduled catering a year in advance, so they too were booked for the full year.

"How's that good news?" Rose said. "We schedule monthly events, and you're scheduled for the full month of June?"

"Ms. Rose, not to worry, Frank mentioned that you're getting married on June first, which will work out," Chef Brew said. He often called Big Eaze Frank because they were good friends. "That day, yes, we do have an event scheduled, but I will have half the staff cater that event and fly the other half to your event. I don't want you to worry. We have enough staff to cover both events because we now have a staff of well over fifty employees. This is a big day for you and Frank. I was not able to recommend anyone, so I see fit that I cater it. What's on the menu?" asked Chef Brew. "Better yet, send it via e-mail, and I'll pull up a shopping cart filled with the items needed for that joyous day."

No one wanted Rose to worry. That had been addressed many times by Big Eaze, who had informed his staff to not ever say no to Rose. He had stressed, time and time again, that it would not be tolerated.

"Oh, thank you, Chef Brew. You are the best, and I am honored to have you on our staff," Rose said. She was now feeling a lot of stress being taken off her shoulders.

After getting off the phone, she decided to take a swim in her pool and have a cold glass of tropical berry tea.

Chapter 16

Measurements

Rose and the Divas, along with Bubbles, were scheduled to be fitted for their dresses at Carlotta's Designs that Friday. They all arrived on time in their separate cars, one being Scarlet's white Range Rover. Ruby's was a black-on-black Maserati. Rose drove her silver Mercedes Benz sedan.

She loved to drive that car whenever she got the chance. She pulled in the parking lot, whipping it into a spot. All eyes were on Rose as she stepped out of her car, dressed in her fitted black jeans and off-the-shoulder black ruffle top. She was sporting her black and leopard cat frames. She was wearing her custom-made black pearl earrings, necklace, and bracelet that was given to her as a birthday gift from her close friend's slash business partners in Nigeria. Her diamond ring, one of the rarest diamonds in the country, was bling on top of bling, and her shoes? Well, let's just say that they were leopard ankle boots. She smiled at the Divas as she retrieved her black Chanel purse and leopard wrap.

"Woo, girl! Get it," Ruby exclaimed. "Where you coming from?"

"Had a lunch meeting with Big Eaze and possibly a new client," Rose said.

"What this time?" asked Scarlet, looking very spectacular herself in her white fitted jeans that were tapered at the ankle. They allowed her to show off her three-karat diamond ankle bracelet. She wore a slim-fitted, striped blue shirt. Her white diamond-encrusted wristlet dangled from her wrist. Scarlet had just gotten in from out of town.

"Umm…let's just say that there are more talks about opening up more restaurants," said Rose.

"Good," said Scarlet. "People love to wine and dine, especially if the chef rocks the menu."

"I second that," said Rose. "Big Eaze has mentioned opening restaurants in Georgia and Connecticut. Let's just say, he and his investment team are looking at a lot of cities right now. Chef Brew will still be the head chef, and we'll be hiring the crew for each restaurant and creating a catering menu that's fitting for each city. In the past year, his staff has significantly grown". "Yeah, you forgot to get back to us, regarding his choice of who should cater the wedding," Ruby said.

"Sorry," said Rose, "but he will be catering the wedding. He could not get anyone on the island to commit. He'll have half the staff stay here, and the other half, he'll take to Barbados."

"Great," Scarlet said. "You are pretty lucky to have a large staff. How many are on board with Chef Brew's staff? DJ Spinn has six DJs on his staff."

"And he's looking to bring in more," Rose said.

"Ha! Diamonds is in need of a larger staff," said Scarlet.

Ruby looked at Scarlet, knowing that Scarlet was out of town on business more than usual, but Ruby didn't say a word. She was pretty much pooped after discussing business with an old friend. She just wanted to get this part of the day over, go home, soak in her tub, and go to bed.

They were greeted with a smile from Carlotta, who thanked them for coming to her shop so late in the day. The shop was closed for the evening. Rose and her family were the last clients of the day. Carlotta was in lockup mode. She welcomed them to tea and assorted cookies, which seemed to have just been baked. They were warm, soft, and gooey.

Rose grabbed a cookie and sat while she waited to be measured and said, "Do you have an oven in here? These cookies are warm."

"Yes," Carlotta confirmed. "Just a small air fryer. I love warm baked cookies." She gave a little laugh as she prepared for the first measurement.

Carlotta's shop had a U-shaped seating area, which was positioned in front of mirrors that provided the perfect view of her clients' front, back, and side. There were lots of magazines with beautiful models wearing the latest fashion designs.

One by one, they were measured from top to bottom, side to side. It took about fifteen minutes to measure each one. Rose was the last one to be measured. As they gathered their things and prepared to leave the shop, Rose asked if everyone would like to stop by the diner down the street for a quick bite to eat.

Ruby said, "No, thanks. I am ready to go home." She asked Bubbles if she wanted to join her G'ma for a bite to eat.

Bubbles said, "No, thanks." She also wanted to go home. She felt like her job was just about over and that she could finally return to a normal life, which would consist of hanging with friends.

So, Rose now turned to Scarlet, who agreed to get a small bite to eat before hanging out with her glam squad from **"Scarlet Kisses"**.

Carlotta thanked Rose for the invite but explained that she would be staying in to start the gowns. She was so excited to be finally starting to sew the gowns. After Rose picked out the right color, she planned, after going over the measurements, to get started right away. She had set goals and did not want to be distracted from her goals, other than going to school. Carlotta thought, after these gowns, I have five dresses to make, along with four couture garments to design. Because there are a lot of details being added to the couture apparel, I'll be pretty busy. She wanted to stay focused on her goals and told Rose that she would have to pass on the invite but thanked Rose for inviting her.

She watched them get in their cars and pull out of the parking lot while turning on a dim light in her front window, which was set on a timer to go off at about two in the morning.

Carlotta designed a window display that had a model mannequin wearing a form-fitted fuchsia gown that flowed with ruffles along the bottom of the dress. She held on tight to her gold purse. She also could be seen in a fuchsia hat that had a feather on its side. The background in the window was set in a vintage time warp. She appeared to be coming or going on a train ride, and the train station that she was walking in had this old-time flare with people coming and going, all dressed in fancy clothing.

Carlotta was ready to get down to business, so she set the garments on her long table and took the measurements for each person, starting with Rose. She grabbed a piece of white chalk and started to create the pattern.

Rose's Story

    Carlotta was in her happy mode, singing and humming to her own music. As she prepared to cut the first garment, she pulled out her very sharp shears, held them high above her head, and spoke to the shears, "Create your masterpiece, Carlotta." Then, she started to cut the garment. The sounds of the shears cutting the fabric could be heard throughout the small shop.

***

By eleven o'clock that evening, Carlotta had the first dress cut out and had placed it on a dress form. She pulled the dress close to her and twirled as if she were dancing at a ball, along with a hundred guests, all dressed in ballroom attire.

    Because it was Friday, Carlotta believed that she could get all four dresses cutout that evening, so she continued throughout the night, singing and humming to her own music.

    She started on the next dress, continuing the same method as the first dress, drawing out the pattern and cutting the material.

***

At one o'clock in the morning, she finally finished the fourth dress. She cleaned up all the material that had fallen on the floor and put them all in a basket for future use. She didn't waste any material. She always found a use for them all.

    By three o'clock in the morning, she was ready to prepare for bed. The back room was set up for sleeping quarters. She'd had ask Rose to add a Murphy bed and a nightstand with a small lamp.

    She pulled down the mattress, which stayed snug into the wall until it was to be used, and, got into bed, and turned the light off. She said her prayers, with much gratitude, thanking God for blessing her so richly.

Before falling asleep, Carlotta was restless. She told herself, "Carlotta, calm down. Get some rest. You have to open up the shop in the morning."

She took deep breaths, turned on some relaxing music, and fell fast asleep.

Chapter 17

A Second Fitting

BETWEEN OPENING AND CLOSING HOURS, Carlotta had been working on the gowns for Rose.

Carlotta now had patrons coming into the shop to see what she had to offer. Some brought material, and some just stayed in to chat and to get to know the new business owner in their community.

Carlotta loved getting to know the people in the community, but she was pressed for time. She was determined to win the hearts of Rose and her clients.

It was past seven o'clock in the evening, and Carlotta had not eaten since late morning. "I'm starving," Carlotta said.

"I must get a bite to eat. I'm feeling a bit famished."

While closing up the shop for the night, Carlotta walked to her fridge that she'd brought a few weeks ago. She'd decided to purchase the fridge because she knew that she would be working late hours at the shop and wouldn't always have time to run to the grocery store during the day. She opened it up to see that all she had were a few pieces of fruit, some milk, and some bread and butter.

Oh, my! thought Carlotta. It is too late to go grocery shopping now. What can I make out of these few items?

She went to open the door of her small pantry where she had enough room to store a few bags of pasta and a couple of canned goods.

She became excited. She had one bag of egg noodles, a can of peas, and one small can of cream of chicken soup.

"Great," she exclaimed. "I'll be making cream chicken noodle soup this evening."

There was no chicken in the can, just flavored chicken. Once the soup was done, she danced her way back to the fridge to get herself a slice of bread to make toast. Then, she added some butter and sprinkled a dash of dry parsley to garnish her noodles. She sat in silence, admiring her so real new surroundings. She smiled at her achievement and thought, I've got to do better, if I'm planning on saving money and working all day. I have to shop. I can't continue to order out. I'll call Evelyn on Sunday and ask for a ride to the grocery store.

"But for now," she said out loud, "I'll eat this delicious meal. Then, I must get back to work."

Carlotta had very little details left to do on the gowns, but she wanted Rose and the Divas to come in for a second fitting.

While she continued eating her dinner, Carlotta noticed that her cell phone was across the room of the shop. It was sitting on her cutting table. Her phone had lit up. By the time she reached her phone, the light went dim.

She noticed that Rose had called and that she had missed four of her calls.

Rose's Story

"Oh, my! This doesn't look good for me." She then noticed that her cell phone ringer was off.

Carlotta immediately called Rose back, but the call went to voice mail.

Carlotta left a voice message.

"Hi, Rose! This is Carlotta. I apologize for missing your calls. My phone was on silent, which I noticed while I was sitting down for dinner. I am at the shop. in case you need to stop by or if you are checking on the status of the gowns. I have pretty much completed cutting and sewing them, but I would like a second fitting. If you can tell me what would be a good day and time for you and the Divas, that would be very much appreciated. I am looking to be completed with all four gowns within a week. Thanks, and again, I apologize for missing your calls and look forward to hearing from you soon."

Carlotta hung up the phone and immediately felt down about missing four of Rose's calls, not one but four. "O-M-G! That does not look good for me. I'm just starting out, and Rose is a huge client."

***

Four hours had gone by, and Carlotta had not heard from Rose until midnight. She kept her phone close to make sure that she did not miss another of Rose's calls.

Carlotta's phone was ringing, which was Rose calling her back. Carlotta answered the phone as fast as she could and immediately started to apologize again.

Rose was silent. She let Carlotta speak, and then she said, "Don't worry yourself. You are a business woman, and there will be missed calls, possibly missed deadlines, and you may run late to meetings.

Things come up.

I went from meetings to luncheons the whole entire day, and look, I'm just getting back to you at twelve a.m., of all hours. Our day should have ended, and we should be sleeping at this hour. It's all in a day of business."

Rose continued, "I just wanted to check up on you, not only on the progress of the gowns, but I also wanted to check to see if you're doing okay and if you needed anything. You're working so hard, Carlotta, and you're working alone. It's not like you have a staff of employees working on the gowns. I'm just concerned."

"Thanks, Ms. Rose, but I'm doing well. I was making dinner when I missed your calls." Carlotta never did mention that she needed to go grocery shopping to Rose. "But yes, I would like to set up a second fitting, this week, if we can. Again, I believe I will be done with all four gowns this week."

"Great," Rose exclaimed. "I sent Scarlet and Ruby a text after I got your message, and they both would like to schedule the fitting on next Tuesday at four p.m. Can you fit us in?"

"Of course," Carlotta said, and she recited the day and time to Rose and thanked her for getting back to her.

"Great! We will see you then, if not before," Rose said. "It's late. Have a good night."

Carlotta thanked Rose again while smiling as she laid down to fall asleep, feeling very much appreciated.

Chapter 18

A Lot Going On

Rose was feeling upbeat. Things seemed to be lining up. The gowns were done a little earlier than she had expected. She had become really close to Carlotta and never doubted that she would not be done with the gowns at the scheduled time. She believed that Carlotta was a hard-working, young woman who was hungry for her startup and that she would be successful in the world of design. That was why she'd hired Carlotta as her personal seamstress and had introduced her to her family, friends, and her close network of business partners. Rose believed in Carlotta from the start. When she opened up the shop for Carlotta, it was not just for the six-month trial but for as long as she was willing to stay focused and continue her dream of owning a shop. Carlotta's next goal was to have a staff of tailors and seamstresses to handle the overflow of work that she believed would be coming in the near future.

***

In the meantime, Chef Brew was in close contact with Rose regarding the wedding menu that consisted of Rose's seafood selections. The food was brought in advance and would be delivered to the villa days before the wedding. Chef Brew had a staff of twenty assigned to fly to Barbados two weeks in advance. He left instructions with his assistant chef on what was to be expected for the two weeks that he would not be in house.

Rose had it set up that they would rent two homes on Crane Beach that would house ten in each home, and Chef Brew would have an offsite hotel suite for himself and his family.

Rose was busy on her computer, getting the final details in order, when Big Eaze came into her office. She looked up and said, "Yes … how can I help you?"

Big Eaze sat down and told Rose that they would need to get ready to fly out to Santa Monica for the ribbon-cutting ceremony.

"Okay," Rose said, but deep down inside, she was not ready for this trip.

She just wanted to concentrate on one thing at a time. Rose was feeling the pressure of keeping up with the demands of Big E's Enterprises, which was growing by leaps and bounds. She never felt as if she really retired.

Rose asked Big Eaze, "What day? And will Sam be handling the travel arrangements?"

Big Eaze assured Rose that all was taken care of and that he was just letting her know that the ceremony was coming up soon.

Rose then said, "Well, don't forget that we are getting married on June first."

Big Eaze chuckled. "Yeah, it's hard not to notice with everyone running around for you in this house. The ribbon cutting is the first weekend in May, and we will leave soon after, which gives us three weeks before the wedding on June first."

"Yeah, which is not enough of time," Rose exclaimed. "For one, we must get our gowns to the villa, the food preparation, the decorations, and the music."

Rose was now showing her distaste for the constant demands of Big E's Enterprises being first in their everyday life. Big Eaze assured Rose that all would go like clockwork when they got back. "You will have all the staff, ready for what is needed to be ready for that spectacular day." Big Eaze reached out to hug Rose, to assure her that he knew that their wedding day was a very special day and that their business, also, was just as important.

Rose was feeling a little better knowing that Big Eaze was not just going with the flow but also had their wedding in mind.

"Okay. Can we go to dinner now?" he asked, looking at Rose for approval.

"Yeah, but we're eating here at home tonight. I am not up to getting dressed for going out to eat," said Rose.

"Okay by me," Big Eaze said as he walked out of Rose's office.

Rose shut down her computer and followed Big Eaze to the kitchen where Evelyn had made them a fresh tossed salad, topped with blackened sea bass fish. They sat down to eat out in their private outdoor covered patio. As they settled in their seats, Rose poured a cold glass of white wine for each of them. Then, she sat back and enjoyed the sunset and the sound of crickets. She looked over at Big Eaze and thought, I will soon be Mrs. Frank Zaiders. Should I keep Crystal, my last name, or take on his name? Rose had not mentioned it, and she would have rather not talked about it at that moment. She just wanted to sit there together and enjoy their dinner on that quiet, peaceful evening.

Big Eaze struck up a conversation about the restaurant opening in Santa Monica. After viewing a slide show on his phone of the restaurant while eating dinner, he told Rose that he thought that she had done an excellent job decorating the place, inside and out.

"Thank you," she said. "I just thought of our place here and how much we love this place, so why not incorporate some of the details into our first restaurant? I'm kind of excited about seeing the place in real time."

"Yeah," Big Eaze said. "It's going to be a big event. The Lomontes' team has assured me that they will have Rosedale Drive shut down for several hours with security. We're going to serve food and beverages and have music with a live circus show after the ribbon-cutting ceremony."

"Oh, yeah," Rose said. "Are we attending that as well, seeing as how we must be back that evening for the grand opening of the restaurant?"

Big Eaze gave Rose the look, which she already knew meant that he would be working.

Chapter 19

Rehearsal Dinner

Scarlet and Ruby had scheduled the wedding rehearsal dinner for the Sunday before leaving out for the ribbon-cutting ceremony in Santa Monica. They all knew that they had a very short window to have the dinner before leaving out, and to top it off, Rose gave the Divas a very long guest list.

After looking over the list Rose gave her, Ruby said, "There's no way that we'll have the time to fit this dinner in once we return from California and especially not with this long list."

Ruby handed Scarlet the massive list that Rose had given her.

The dinner was catered by their very own Chef Brew, which allowed Evelyn and her staff to rest that evening and be a part of the dinner. Evelyn would not sit down because she kept giving orders to the hired staff. No one dared to say a word to Evelyn. They just let her be, even Rose could not sit her down.

The dinner consisted of lamb chops, roasted red potatoes, green beans that were garnished with freshly sliced garlic and red grape tomatoes. There was lots of white wine being served.

Scarlett and Ruby, along with Bridgette, had planned to have the garden set up as a replica of Crane Beach where Rose planned to wed in Barbados.

The gazebo was used as the canopy that Rose and Big Eaze, along with the priest, would stand under. The seating areas were formed in an oval shape, which wrapped behind the gazebo on its separate deck.

The guests were seated very comfortably on plush throw pillows. The lighting on both decks gave off a soft glow, which lit up the pond and seemed to twinkle against the ripples in the water.

Before the dinner was served, everyone sat in the designated seats to watch Rose and Big Eaze practice their lines. Rose seemed to be a bit nervous. She kept forgetting her lines. She finally got through it to give Big Eaze a chance, and he did just that. He nailed it like a champ.

After Rose and Big Eaze were done with their lines, everyone was directed to their seating area in the garden, and they were all served that delicious meal.

DJ Spinn was on the spin table, kicking off, once again, the hottest hits.

After dinner, everyone got up out of their seats, and they danced, laughed, and joked until about midnight.

The Divas were happy that the pre-wedding rehearsal dinner had been flawless. During the rehearsal dinner, they found out that most of the guests would not be at the actual wedding.

Rose had told the Divas that she and Big Eaze had a dozen set of friends and all could not be in one place at one time and the guests that attended the pre-wedding dinner were their business partners/ friends that would be out of the country on business but did not want to miss the wedding rehearsal.

"It's all about networking. You've got to keep everyone happy," said Rose.

That Wednesday, Rose, Big Eaze, Scarlet, Ruby, and the investment team of four men flew to Santa Monica. Evelyn, also, went on this trip because Rose would not travel without her at this time. They all boarded their plane to Santa Monica at mid-morning.

They had planned an early morning flight, but their flight had been delayed for an hour.

Bubbles stayed back home with Sam because she was still in school and had prior commitments that she could not miss.

Chapter 20

Opening up a Restaurant

Rose, Big Eaze, the Divas, Evelyn, and the investment team flew to Santa Monica, California, for the opening of the new restaurant named Lomontes'. It was such a big deal. The event was televised, and it was being reported as the newest, hippest, trendiest restaurant to open in Santa Monica. This was all because of the Lomontes' management team and their entire staff. They had hit the pavement hard and had networked that year, getting the restaurant's name out on a large scale. They'd hosted parties, had live TV shows, and commercials announcing that the new restaurant would open that year in mid-spring on Rosedale Drive.

They all arrived at the Lidos Hotel and, not long after, they were whisked away in a limo for the ribbon-cutting ceremony. Their flight had been delayed for an hour, and Rose felt like she had not had enough time to get properly dressed, so she was annoyed. She took out her mirror from her purse and made sure that her hair and makeup were still on fleek.

After primping in the mirror, Rose was pleased with her hair and

Rose's Story

makeup. She calmed herself down, wrapped a smile on her face, and got ready for anything that came her way.

As they arrived at the restaurant, the limo parked in the restaurant parking lot, taking up about four spaces. Big Eaze looked over at Rose and asked if she would like to hand out business cards to anyone that may be standing out in front of the restaurant witnessing the ribbon-cutting ceremony.

Lomontes' logo was the French doors of the restaurant. The business cards featured the logo with the name of the restaurant printed above the doors in fancy letters written in metallic gold. Without a second thought, Rose took the cards, and the door opened to the limo. As they all got out of the limo, Rose saw a crowd of people in front of the restaurant, hanging over the white benches, looking to see who had arrived in the stretch black Mercedes limo.

As she approached the crowd standing near the restaurant, Rose did not recognize a single face, but she waved and smiled and gave out the business cards, saying "Hello, hello, hello! Thank you for coming to the ribbon-cutting ceremony."

Ruby, Scarlet, and Rose stood next to Big Eaze, along with the investment team of four men (Richard, Bob, Ethan and Earl) and the Lomontes' management team. They were all holding on to a thick shiny metallic gold ribbon.

Big Eaze and his team of investors, along with Lomontes' management team, were given huge plastic scissors as they were instructed at the count of three to cut the ribbon simultaneously.

"One! Two! Three!" the crowd shouted.

The ribbon was cut in half.

Then, pop, pop, pop. The popping of confetti cans followed, and soon the confetti rained down on their heads. Rose looked up to see waves of confetti gently blowing against the wind.

Music blasted from tall speakers that sat near the front entrance of the restaurant, which, by the way, was designed by Rose to look very much like the front entrance of the Crystal Manor.

The entrance boasted large cream pillars with shrubs in planters that sat next to the front doors of the restaurant. The French doors were lined in cream color, and the glass was tinted black and were accented with cream draperies. The lighting was in recess, and it gave off a warm feeling, like going home for dinner, but also showed style and class.

Trays of finger food were wheeled out and given to the crowds of people standing there, witnessing the ribbon ceremony. It was like a block party; the police had shut down the block so that no cars would come up or down the street for the next few hours.

The Lomontes' team of workers had a circus ring-like theme, there with people on tall wooden legs walking around, twirling long colored ribbons while magical acts were being conducted, and several men and women were juggling fruit and not one hit the ground. A long table was being set up that continued to serve finger foods, fruit bowls, slices of cake, and beverages to the crowd. More and more people came to see what was happening on Rosedale Drive.

Soon after the ribbon-cutting ceremony, Rose left the event to get some rest for the grand opening that evening. It sure was going to be crowded with people. Sam had given Big Eaze a list of people that would be attending the grand opening. The people on this list would be seated in the VIP seating area. These people were the A-list people that lived in Santa Monica, from the mayor to CEOs of companies in

Rose's Story

the Santa Monica valley. They would all dine at Lomontes', which the team believed was the best cuisine in Santa Monica, and they hoped they would give a good name to the restaurant.

Big Eaze and his investment team planned on opening more restaurants in the states of California, Georgia, New York, and Connecticut, so he also wanted this night to be a success.

After some much-needed rest, Rose pinned her hair and soaked in a long, hot, rose milk bath. They had hours to get ready for the grand opening, which would possibly go well into the early hours of the morning.

Rose needed the rest, and rest she got. She instructed for there to be scented vanilla filters in the room and for the room to be set at a cool setting with soft instrumental music played by Peter White and Brian Culbertson, who were two of Rose's favorite Jazz musicians. All of this was done for Rose's routine mediation, which she believed really helped her during long days and nights when Big E's Enterprises hosted events.

Now Big Eaze was not there to take in the setup that Rose had created. He was out in meetings, going over last-minute details. Ruby was right there by his side, which helped her learn more about the restaurant side of the business. Scarlet had gone out shopping for a new dress to wear to the grand opening ceremony. After what she saw at the ribbon-cutting ceremony, she thought that she needed to step up her game.

***

Later that evening, Rose's alarm went off. She saw that she had been asleep for a few hours. It was now time to prepare for the evening event.

While getting out of bed, she noticed Big Eaze was fully dressed. He was sitting at the table with his laptop open and phone in hand. Rose thought, He's still at it. I wonder if he's even gotten any sleep.

After her makeup was done and Evelyn had helped her with her gown, Rose looked back at Evelyn and said, "Don't you bail on me tonight. Get dressed, Evelyn. We are going on a date."

Evelyn did not fuss but went back to her room and got dressed in a gown that she had wanted to wear for a long time. She put on her pumps and pranced in front of the mirror while thinking, Looking good there, lady.

***

After arriving in their limos, they graced the red carpet. Cameras with LED lighting flashed in their eyes. As they walked the red carpet, lights above their heads were beaming down on them from a news helicopter covering the grand opening.

Rose was wearing a long, gold sequined gown that shimmered in the lights. Her gold red bottom sling back sandals could barely be seen. Her hair was pinned up in a bun. She dazzled the crowd with her teardrop sparkling diamond earrings, while holding Big Eaze's hand. Big Eaze looked very handsome in a black tux with a bow tie. He was sporting a fresh cut and a pair of black leather Gucci slip-on shoes.

Someone in the crowd yelled out, "Gucci!"

Ruby graced the red-carpet, wearing a fitted black Versace gown. She stopped and smiled while pictures of her were taken. She was approached by a journalist who asked her, "Aren't you Ruby Crystal, the investment mogul? Are you a co-owner of Lomontes'?" She was holding the mic in Ruby's face.

Rose's Story

Ruby smiled but did not give into the demands of the journalist because she did not want to take away from Big E's Enterprises' first restaurant grand opening. Ruby thought, this is not for me but for my family. So, she continued on toward the front entrance.

Scarlet was not too far behind. She laced the red carpet in a Valentino silk black gown and was, of course, wearing her signature red lipstick. She had **"Scarlet Kisses"** written all over her, and of course, the same journalist approached Scarlet saying, "I finally get to meet the famous **"Scarlet Kisses"**. You are known all over Paris."

Scarlet smiled as pictures of her were taken. She, also, did not give much of a glance to the journalist and continued on toward the front entrance of the restaurant, where they would all to take a group picture.

As the hired photographer wrapped up taking pictures, Big Eaze walked toward the crowd and thanked them all for allowing him and his family to walk the carpet in a respectful manner, without incident, and hoped that they would soon come to the restaurant and take in a great meal.

He then turned toward his family, and the French doors to the restaurant opened, and they walked into Lomontes' for their very first dinner.

The layout of restaurant's dining area was a bright open floor plan, with filtered overhead lanterns, giving off a romantic atmosphere. Each table was laced with white silk linen and floating wax candles draped in white roses. It was superb. The white tall back chairs looked very comfortable.

There was a live band playing soft jazz that evening.

Rose, Big Eaze, Scarlet, and Ruby, along with Evelyn and the investors and the Lomontes' team, were guided to their expansive table. Champagne bottles were being brought to their table as they all sat in their designated seats.

Rose looked over at Big Eaze and showed her approval of the place. She quietly took in a deep breath and whispered to Big Eaze, "It smells like vanilla in here," and smiled as she continued to look around and be pleased with the setup.

Not too long after, more guests that were invited to sit in the VIP area arrived to dine at Lomontes'.

When Big Eaze saw that the VIPs were coming in, he and his team immediately got up to personally thank them for their support. Big Eaze asked if anyone wanted any champagne. "Dom Perignon, to be exact. Please let the host know and add it to my tab."

As they chatted a bit, he mentioned that he did not want to keep them from a wonderful dining experience, along with great jazz. "Oh, I must not forget, for dessert, they are serving slices of warm apple crumb pie made with the finest ingredients from a local bakery in town. We're not too far from you. So, if you would need anything please, please don't hesitate to ask your host."

Big Eaze and his team thanked them and headed back to their table.

Chapter 21

Party into the A.M.

The dinner party lasted well into the a.m. Rose, Evelyn, and the Divas had left the restaurant about midnight. Before leaving, Rose gave Big Eaze a kiss goodnight and whispered in his ear.

He walked them out to an awaiting limo and said to the driver, "Be careful. We have rare, precious jewels on board." He closed the door to the limo, and the driver drove off.

While walking back into the restaurant, Big Eaze noticed a young man sitting on some steps to an adjacent building near the restaurant. The young man was wearing a wireless headset and was rapping to whatever he was listening to.

Big Eaze listened intently and was impressed with the young man's rap flow. He stopped before entering the restaurant, then walked toward where the young man was sitting.

Big Eaze's bodyguard put his hand on his shoulder to stop him from going toward the young man, but Big Eaze assured his bodyguard that he was okay.

Rock asked, "You sure, boss? You're not from this city."

"I got this," said Big Eaze. He approached the rapper and asked, "What's your name, young man?"

The young man pulled his headset off, looked Big Eaze up and down, and said, "Excuse me?"

"What's your name?" asked Big Eaze.

"Why? I'm not in the way. I'm sitting here waiting for my girlfriend to get off work," said the young man.

"Cool. I respect that," said Big Eaze, "but you still didn't give me your name."

The young man chuckled and said, "JB. My name JB, and why you ask?"

Well, Big Eaze found himself sitting next to JB, rapping about the music industry and how he was looking for new talent to join his team.

"What does JB stand for, and are you from Cali?" asked Big Eaze.

JB stood proud, his chest stuck out, smiled, and said, "JB stands for Javon Brown, and nope, I'm from Miami, Florida."

Big Eaze chuckled. "Aww! All right, so she got you up here in the valley. What you do for work?"

"I work for a messenger company. I study music and rap on the weekends," he said.

"Yeah, keep this one going. You'll get far," said Big Eaze. "I'd like to invite you to come to my studio and hang out with my music manager, DJ. Spinn. He's a great mentor." He handed JB a business card. "Yo! Be safe and call my office, so we can set up that visit."

JB took the business card and looked at the address. His eyes got really big as he thought, Wow, I just spoke to one of the biggest names in the music industry.

Rose's Story

Big Eaze went back into the restaurant and was greeted by the remaining guests, who all appeared to be businessmen and businesswomen. One by one, they came to their table, took a seat, and chatted about Santa Monica and what they had planned for the valley.

Big Eaze was all ears and so was his investment team. They listened to each one talk about renovations, new building sites, bringing in more beachfront homes, and store-front communities.

"You came in at the right time" said the mayor of Santa Monica. "Hope that we are able to meet your expectations as a business owner and possibly bring in more business to the valley."

Big Eaze stood to shake the mayor's hand and to thank him for dining at Lomontes'. It was one in the morning. The restaurant was closed for the evening, and the employees were cleaning up for the next day, which would be the first time that the general public would dine at the restaurant.

Before they were able to clean their sections, Big Eaze called them all together to thank them for all their hard work. He said, "Keep this up and there'll be some bonuses to go out."

The staff cheered, thanking Big Eaze for the pep talk. They went on their way, talking and laughing, giving each other high fives. The staff of twenty were to return that evening for the general public's introduction to Lomontes'. The hours of operations were from 5:00 p.m. to 12:00 a.m.

Big Eaze and his investment team had moved their seats to a smaller table to conduct business before leaving that Monday morning. Each expressed how they felt the evening had gone.

"The real test will come when the general public comes in," Big Eaze said. "We feeling comfortable?" He looked at his team.

They all agreed, believing that they had a pretty good, stable team working at Lomontes'.

Bob said, "They pretty much covered the valley with their intensive networking."

"Yeah, you seen the media? We should be talked about in homes, companies, clubs, and parties. I feel good about this investment," Richard said.

"Likewise," said Ethan.

"What about you, Earl? You got any feedback. You're sitting there all quiet," said Big Eaze.

"Yo! I'm good. Just cut the check," Earl said in his deep voice.

"Yo!" Big Eaze chuckled at Earl's comment. "Check this dude. About two months ago you were up in arms about where this team was. Now you want checks."

A rapture of laughter filled the restaurant.

"Ah, man, we all was shaken up about this deal," Earl said between laughs.

"Yeah, you right. I thought we were being catfished!" said Big Eaze.

"Catfished? What? I was like, no, he didn't say we were catfished, like a blind date," said Richard, who was the closest to Big Eaze, more like a brother. They'd grown up in the same community, had gone to the same schools, and had played basketball and football together.

They were so loud with all the laughing that the staff looked in their direction and started laughing with them.

One staff member said, "I like those dudes. They seem to be a down-to-earth, cordial, respectful, and upstanding group of men … real bosses."

Rose's Story

***

At three in the morning, the last to leave the restaurant was Mitch the manager of the restaurant, who was a really quiet man. He was a very educated and down to business type of man. He worked hard and took his role serious. He wanted to make sure all was ready for the next day.

Big Eaze had noticed Mitch when he would shop at his favorite clothing shop. They became close because Mitch would pay very close attention to details and was always able to help Big Eaze find what he was looking for.

Mitch knew what Big Eaze's taste in clothes was. He'd spent a lot of time with Big Eaze and his investment friends. They tipped Mitch well.

Big Eaze admired Mitch's work ethic, and once he knew that the restaurant was a real, solid deal, Big Eaze proposed a manager position to him, letting him know that it was for a new restaurant being built in California.

Mitch was not married and did not have a steady girlfriend, so it was easy for Big Eaze to propose the position, with a good salary that included a fully furnished apartment and rent paid for a year. Mitch could not let this opportunity pass, and Big Eaze was happy to have him on his team.

Chapter 22

Beach Party in Barbados

Rose was feeling good, and all appeared to be going like clockwork, as Big Eaze had promised that it would. They were packed and ready for their trip to Barbados. Big Eaze had hired a pilot and a co-pilot, along with renting a Boeing airline jet, to fly the catering staff, Chef Brew and his family, Rose, Scarlet, Ruby, Bubbles, Evelyn, Sam, and DJ Spinn and his staff down to Barbados. Carlotta would be on standby if needed.

The wedding was in two weeks, and there was still so much to do to prepare for the wedding. The day that they arrived, Chef Brew prepared a party at the rental homes on Crane Beach. Both homes were adjacent to each other, which allowed for an easy flow to the entertaining. Each rental home had five bedrooms, three baths, a massive kitchen, and a dining room that overflowed into the living room.

For entertainment, the home came with an eighty-inch Mitsubishi television screen, which was hooked up to a camera viewing the beach front.

Rose's Story

DJ Spinn had set up a volleyball net and had organized everyone into two teams of eight on each side. No one professed to be a pro at volleyball, so there was sand being lifted and thrown everywhere. They played a set of three.

While everyone played volleyball, Rose sat on the porch of one of the homes with a book in hand, trying to relax her mind and body. She was a little tense after their travels from California, along with a short stay at home, and then off to Barbados. It was a lot in one week, not to mention all the meetings and promoting and dinner parties…event after event after event. Rose let out a sigh of what she would sum up to be a temporary relief. Then, she thought, I need a vacation from all this constant going here, there, and everywhere. Where will I go, and who will I bring? Surely not Frank. He's always working.

Rose had found herself calling Big Eaze by his first name more often. Oh, yeah! I know. I'll plan an all-inclusive women's retreat to Aruba or Greece. No…to the Fiji Islands…Heck! Anywhere where we can unplug our electronic devices and become one with nature. Frank might be upset at first, but knowing him, he'll find a way to get in contact with me. Heck! He needs this as much as I do.

Rose had not seen Big Eaze standing in front of her holding a tall glass of white wine along with a seafood salad sandwich, which had lobster spilling out on its sides. She laughed. "You look like you're on vacation." She looked at Big Eaze from head to toe. He was dressed in oversize tan Bermuda shorts but had on a white dress shirt and was sporting Nike flip flop sandals. Wow! What a view, thought Rose.

Big Eaze said, "You know I love to come down here and spend a couple days at the villa, take those long walks on the beach, listen to the waves crash. I get very relaxed when we come here, Rose."

Rose looked at Big Eaze. She was really happy to finally see him relax. She said, "Well, don't get too relaxed. You are in a wedding."

The night fell fast, causing the volleyball game to come to an end. After packing up the net, the men found some firepits in the homes, so a fire was set to make s'mores. They played music and coerced Big Eaze and Rose into dancing around the fire.

After the two were tired of dancing, they sat down with the others and listened as Chef Brew told spooky stories that didn't make much sense. One story was about a mermaid who came on shore and sat with a shipwrecked crew of pirates. They sat around a huge wood fire, made from some of their wrecked ship, and ate chili hotdogs on peanut butter bagel rolls.

Another one of his stories was about when he had catered for a bicyclist club that was hosting a night bike race on the beach. They had to ride their bikes as close to the water as possible, and they were doing this at full speed under a moonlit sky, and the winner would receive a year's supply of motor oil.

Bubbles said, "Motor oil? They were riding bikes."

Chef Brew said, "Oh, well, that was the winning prize."

Rose and Big Eaze got up from their spot on the beach and thanked the crew for coming out on such short notice. They let the crew know that they appreciated all that they were doing for them to make their day a special day.

Rose said that she considered them family and hoped they felt the same. She said, "Over the next two weeks, we will be very busy. I hope that you all get plenty of rest, but don't forget to have fun. You're in Barbados for God's sake. But we will need for you to be available to do whatever is asked of you in preparation for our big day. Again, thank

Rose's Story

you so very much!"

For the staff, during their two-week stay, Rose had stocked the fridge and the cabinets with food, beverages, and snacks. She went on to tell the staff, "If you want to dine out, it's on your expense."

Chase, Big Eaze and Rose's driver, was also flown down on that Boeing airline jet, who sat close to Sam, chit chatting the whole entire flight. Had arrived in Big Eaze's triple black Lexani Mesh Grille Range Rover Sport truck. After parking, he got out and opened the back door of the truck so that Rose and Big Eaze could get comfortable in the back seat. He asked, "Where to, boss?" while looking at Rose and Big Eaze to lead the way.

Big Eaze said, "To the villa, we go, my man."

It was a quiet, relaxing ride to the villa.

They sat back and enjoyed their fifteen-minute ride as they viewed the moonlit coastline and admired the moon's reflection that hovered over the open sea, and the smell of salty ocean water.

Big Eaze said, "You tell me that you can't get used to this every evening?"

Rose, after hearing Big Eaze's comment, turned to look at his face and thought, what is this about? He really loves being here in Barbados. Could this be a permanent residence?

Rose turned back to look at that gorgeous moonlit sky.

When they arrived at the villa, Big Eaze got out of the truck first, opened the door for Rose, and they walked into their picturesque villa. The villa was made to look like it was floating above the ocean.

Once inside the villa, Big Eaze stretched his arms out and yelled, "Home, sweet home!"

Rose looked at him and said, "What? This is not home."

"Yes, it is. It's one of many," he said while sitting down on their wrap-around leather chase sofa.

The house was furnished in a tropical theme with high ceilings and tall glass windows and palm tree plants that brought in the whole view of the ocean.

"Whenever we buy a home, it's our home," said Big Eaze.

"I guess you're right. I just consider the manor to be our home, and any other place is a place to stay while we're there on business. That is what we do when we visit the other homes."

"We conduct business meetings, schedule dinner parties, and of course, you want me to be right there by your side."

Rose wanted to mention her all-inclusive women's retreat but decided to wait until after the wedding.

They had not mentioned a honeymoon trip.

Big Eaze just stared at Rose and finally said, "I'm sorry if our businesses call for most of our attention. We would not have all of this …" Big Eaze pointed out things in the home. "…if it wasn't for our businesses."

Rose said, "True. But all of our attention? Come on. It's not necessary. You should have others in place to do their parts."

"I do," Big Eaze said.

"Yeah, and you got to be a part of that as well."

"Hey, my crew … we're like brothers, and the businesses that we have, you have to be very close to your 'brothers' partners. Look at Evelyn. You insist that she travel with you most of the time."

Rose interrupted Big Eaze to say, "Did you hear yourself? Most of the time."

"Well, don't forget the staff at the Manor. You cater to them all of the time."

"They're like family, one that you trust with your life."

Well, that is how I feel about my brothers. I trust them. They trust me. It's been tested," Big Eaze said.

"Yeah, yeah," said Rose as she walked toward the master bathroom to run herself a rose milk bath. After her bath, she would head to bed.

Chapter 23

The Week Goes by Fast

"Once people know you're in town, they'll do whatever they can to grab your attention. But there'd been very little time for any type of distraction while here in the Barbados. There'll be no events, no luncheons, no trade shows, and no business meetings." Rose made sure that Big Eaze understood all of that.

She would call on him to do this and that, anything to keep his mind off work. Big Eaze was instructed to go to the local hardware store to make sure that the canopy was built as what was given to them months ago.

At the hardware store, Big Eaze had his hands full building the deck and the guest seating area, which had grown in size. Big Eaze said to Rose, "I have not worked like this in twenty years. What're you trying to prove, Rose?" He looked curiously at his future wife.

Rose hadn't said a word. By the end of the day, she would run Big Eaze his bath water with Epsom salt with a big grin on her face.

Rose did not have him volunteering every day, just on the days that she caught wind that he was going to a business meeting or invited to a luncheon. Rose was determined to keep his mind focused on the wedding.

***

At ten o'clock in the morning, Scarlet and Ruby walked through the door and smelled the aroma of bacon.

"Umm…" Scarlet said, "did we time breakfast at the right time?"

Evelyn chuckled and asked the Divas if they wanted to have breakfast.

"No," Scarlet said but grabbed a couple pieces of bacon.

"No, thanks" Ruby said, "but if you have some orange juice, I'll take a glass."

"Yes, matter of fact, it's freshly squeezed," Evelyn said while pouring a full glass for Ruby.

"How special is that?" said Ruby as Evelyn handed her the glass full of freshly squeezed orange juice.

Before anyone could ask if Rose was up, she walked into the kitchen, still dressed in her night clothes.

Scarlet said, "What? Why are you not dressed? I thought we all agreed that we would go girl shopping today."

Rose said that she was not feeling well and needed to get more rest. "My body aches, and I have a massive headache, and my eyes are puffy."

Scarlet and Ruby looked at Rose, and Scarlet said, "This is not good. You're getting married in less than five days. What can we get you?"

Rose said, "Nothing. I really think I'm just exhausted, with little time to rest from getting the dresses picked out and the opening of the restaurant and the flight here. I have not had a day to rest. I'm exhausted, and I need a day off. Matter of fact, I'm feeling lightheaded right now." As she finished speaking, Rose fainted.

If it hadn't been for the quick actions of Scarlet, Ruby and Evelyn, Rose would have hit the cold marble floor, hard.

By then, Big Eaze had entered the kitchen and yelled out, "What is going on? Are you okay, Rose?" He grabbed her out of the arms of Ruby and Scarlet and touched her face with the palm of his hands. "What's wrong? Are you okay?"

"I'm okay. I'm just feeling a little tired and light-headed," said Rose. "Please take me back to my room." She stopped and turned back to face the Divas and said, "I'm okay. Don't worry. I just need to rest."

Big Eaze walked back to the kitchen to talk to the Divas who now appeared to be getting all worked up, not knowing what was going on with Rose, but Big Eaze assured them that he would call their doctor to come check in on Rose. He promised that he would call them after the visit.

"Please go about your day, and if there are any changes, I will call you both," Big Eaze said.

Ruby had him promise them that he would not leave Rose's side.

"Of course, I will not leave her side" said Big Eaze.

The Divas did not leave willingly but eventually agreed that Rose needed some extra R&R. Soon after the Divas left out, Big Eaze had Evelyn call their private doctor.

Evelyn immediately retrieved the number to call the office of Dr. Seagrass.

After she spoke with the receptionist, Dr. Seagrass got on the line.

"Hi, Evelyn. How are you?" asked Dr. Seagrass.

"I'm well, but this call is for Rose. She's a little under the weather, and Frank wanted you to make a house call."

"Of course, I will. Please let Frank know that I should be there within an hour."

After hanging up the phone, Evelyn found Big Eaze looking out the tall glass window onto the beach area. "Excuse me, Frank. I was able to speak with Dr. Seagrass. He should be here within an hour."

"Not fast enough," yelled Big Eaze.

Evelyn was startled with this tone in his voice. "His office is about forty-five minutes away," Evelyn pointed out.

Big Eaze turned to face Evelyn and asked, "And how would you know this?"

"Frank, it's my job to know these things. I'm Rose's assistant."

"No, you're the maid," said Big Eaze. "You cook for us. You seem to manage the employees at the Manor. How's that? When you're the maid?"

"I'm no maid," Evelyn said. "I am Rose's personal assistant. It seems you are unaware of this. We've been friends for years. I'm by her side when you're off in meetings, when you're out golfing with your friends. I have known Rose since well before you came into her life. So, if you don't mind, I'll go check in on her."

"Well, I do mind. I'll be checking on my wife," said Big Eaze.

Evelyn walked off rolling her eyes. She went to the kitchen to put away the breakfast food. Afterward, she sat in her room, trying to forget the clashing of Titans between her and Big Eaze.

I really like working for Rose, but if Frank does not take a step back, I'll leave. I demand respect. Rose and I have been friends for well over twenty years. I'll talk to Rose about this and find out what his issue is with me. I've not felt welcome when he's around. Or could it be he feels intimated by our friendship? Evelyn laughed. Well, he'll need to get over it because I'm here to stay, thought Evelyn.

Evelyn heard Dr. Seagrass in the home. She then left her room to see what he had to say about Rose.

While in the kitchen, Evelyn overheard Dr. Seagrass talking to Rose and Big Eaze in their bedroom. Come to find out that Rose was correct. She was exhausted and dehydrated. The doctor advised that she get plenty of rest and drink lots of liquids.

"With all of the constant coming and going, you have to get rest in between your demanding schedule, Rose. If not, it can wreak havoc on your immune system. It's okay for some people to constantly go, and for others, it's not so wise." He continued, "Rose, you know your body better than anyone. So, say no when you're feeling tired. Ask yourself if you are you enjoying the constant coming and going. If not, cut back a little. Have you and your assistant looked over your schedule to see where you can cut back?"

Big Eaze stood there and listened to Dr. Seagrass go over and over the same message.

"We get it, *Seagas!*, Stop repeating yourself!" Big Eaze wanted to say out loud, but he knew Rose would sharply cut her eyes at him. So, he stood there, listening to the same repeated lecture.

Dr. Seagrass turned to look over at Big Eaze and asked, "How are you feeling, Frank?"

Before he could mention another word, Big Eaze said, "I'm well. Is there anything else that we need to give Rose? We are getting married this Saturday, and I want my wife to be—"

Dr. Seagrass cut in and went on to repeat the same message that

Rose's Story

he'd just said to Rose. She sat quietly and listened to her doctor. Rose had chosen Dr. Seagrass for their private doctor when visiting Barbados. His reviews were well with Rose. Dr. Seagrass mentioned that the key was rest, fluids, and exercise. He was now pointing at Big Eaze as he looked back at Rose. He told Rose that she would be fine. "Call me if you need to. I don't want to take up any more of your time."

Rose thanked her doctor for taking time out of his busy schedule. She promised that she would get that much-needed rest.

"Have a great rest of the day, Dr. Seagrass," said Rose.

"Of course. Thank you," Dr. Seagrass said, and Big Eaze showed him out, by walking him toward the kitchen.

Dr. Seagrass saw Evelyn at the kitchen table and immediately went to talk to her.

Big Eaze followed and told Evelyn, "Please see the doctor out while I go back to talk to Rose. Thanks again, doc."

But Dr. Seagrass no longer paid Big Eaze any attention. He was now holding Evelyn's hand, and from what Big Eaze could make out, they were now laughing.

Big Eaze stood there for a few seconds, shook his head, and left their presence while mumbling to himself, "I don't see nothing funny. My wife is not feeling well, and Evelyn has the nerve to be laughing. This is no laughing matter. I'll take care of this and have Rose fire her!"

Big Eaze reached the room and found Rose fast asleep.

Chapter 24

The Key: R&R

Rose slept most of the day. When she did get up, she took a hot shower and had a small dinner and headed back to sleep. Big Eaze tried to get her to talk to him to see how she was feeling. Rose felt the vibe and hurried back to bed. All the while, she was thinking, He just wants to see if it's okay to leave out.

***

The next morning, Rose got up feeling rejuvenated. She had not seen Big Eaze, so she put on her long silk robe and went to see if he was still in the home. Big Eaze was on his phone, and his laptop opened.

Loudly, Rose cleared her throat to let Big Eaze know that she was in the room.

Big Eaze hurried to end his call. "Oh, let me call you guys later. Rose is up and looking in my direction." Big Eaze paused and then said, "Okay. I will let her know." After getting off the phone, he said, "Hey, my beautiful Rose. How are you feeling? And the guys said hello and that they hope you are feeling better."

"What guys?" Rose asked.

"Ethan, Earl, and Richard."

"Oh, did I interrupt a business meeting?"

"No...I mean, yeah, we were catching up on—"

Rose politely interrupted Big Eaze. "I knew it. You can't stand to be away from work for just one week. You're going to run yourself ragged. Or maybe you're just that Energizer Bunny. You keep going and going. I have to cut back on some of the meetings, the events and the luncheons. I need my me-time back," said Rose as she looked at Big Eaze with wide eyes before she turned to walk out of the living room.

But before leaving his sight, she turned back and said, "I'm sure that we will have a lot to do today, and we only have four days before we get married. So, whatever you are trying to plan, whether it be on a conference call, web calling, texting, or the old-fashioned face-to-face meeting, I suggest that you not do it."

Big Eaze just sat there in total silence.

***

Later that day, Rose and Evelyn met up with the Divas to see what needed to be done.

"Hey," Rose said. "I'm feeling rejuvenated." Rose shook her shoulders. "So, what's the plan for today. There's only three and a half days left before my special day." She smiled.

Ruby said, "We pretty much got it all covered. Everything should fall into place. We're putting up the deck the day before the wedding."

"Yes, and there's not much decorating besides the canopy and the seating area. The beach is pretty much our canvas," said Scarlet.

"What about Chef Brew? How is he doing?" asked Rose.

"I'm guessing well. There's been a party every night at the beach homes," said Ruby.

"A party?" asked Rose.

"You know, dinner, games, more of his spooky stories that are far-fetched but funny," said Scarlet.

"Oh, okay." Rose laughed.

"And you? How are you feeling?" asked Scarlet.

Both Divas looked at Rose for a response.

"O-M-G! A lot better … I was so pooped," said Rose.

"Good. You had all of us very worried," said Ruby.

Evelyn was very quiet while out with Rose and the Divas.

"Well, we have a good three and a half days left before I become Mrs. Zaiders, and everything seems to be done. I guess I can continue resting. I can sit on the beach under a canopy and read a good book or write a good book." Rose shrugged her shoulders and looked at everyone, not knowing what to do because there was nothing left to do.

"Yup! Everyone here is playing a part in the wedding, and it's getting done," said Scarlet.

"Oh! I forgot to ask about DJ Spinn. What's he been up to?" Rose laughed. "I'm asking as if I've taken four days off and I've not seen anyone. Did he mention anything about the music that should be played at the wedding?"

"We have not asked because, last you told us, he was well aware of the Caribbean music. So, I'm guessing we are to trust him," said Ruby.

"Yeah, you're right," said Rose.

"Mom, a couple months ago, you gave us a job, to plan your

wedding, because evidently you became frustrated with the process. That's what we're doing, what we do all the time, host events. Yours will be no different … trust us," said Scarlet.

"You're right, girls … I trust you, so what's next?" asked Rose.

They all laughed.

***

Rose, Evelyn, and the Divas went out shopping for those beach sandals. Bubbles did not tag along with the girls on their shopping trip.

Chef Brew's daughter went to the same school as Bubbles. So, Bubbles had been hanging out with Chef Brew and his family, and they all had been hanging out at the beach homes.

Scarlet took the girls to a small boutique on the beach front named Snarled. She had visited that shop, at least, a dozen times while there in Barbados.

As they walked into the shop, they were greeted by the owner. The owner noticed that Scarlet had walk into the shop with three other women.

"Good afternoon, ladies," the tall, handsome man with skin the color of cocoa said. "I'm the owner of Snarled, and I have exactly what you're looking for."

Rose gave the young man a very strange look and said, "How's that? We just walked in."

Scarlet blushed and said, "I've visited this shop many times in the past two weeks, and I've grown fond of many of the things in the shop."

By that time, the owner was handing each one of them the beach sandals that Scarlet had previously picked out.

Scarlet gestured to the tall handsome man and said, "By the way, this is…"

And he said, "Forgive my rudeness. Hello again. I'm Tide, the owner of this shop, and it's a pleasure to finally meet you."

"Oh," said Rose, now smiling and looking in Scarlet's direction. She turned back to Tide and said, "Nice to meet you."

Ruby, also, a little shocked, said, "I'm Ruby, Scarlet's sister. Nice to meet you." After looking over the beach sandals, she said, "These are nice." Then, she looked at Rose.

"Yeah, they are," said Rose, who then looked at Tide. "I'm Rose, Scarlet's mom, if you weren't aware of that."

Tide cut in and said, "I'm very aware of who you are. Scarlet has talked a lot about the wedding soon to be hosted on Crane Beach, a private ceremony. I'm very excited that she has chosen my shop to pick out the beach sandals for you beautiful ladies to wear."

"Well, thank you," said Rose.

Scarlet asked Rose if she approved of the beach shoes, and Rose said, "Yes, I do."

Scarlet now bought four beach sandals, along with some other items, which totaled up to two hundred dollars.

The sandals were wrapped in strings of pearls which made them a perfect match for a Caribbean beach wedding, and they also went well with the accessories worn in the wedding party's hair.

After the purchases, Tide asked if they would like to go to lunch. He mentioned that there was a restaurant not too many shops from his that sold the best lobster salad sandwiches.

Rose remembered Big Eaze standing in front of her with a lobster salad sandwich that had lobster spilling over its bun. "Yes, why not," Rose said.

"I'm up for it as well," said Ruby.

Evelyn still was very quiet while out with Rose, and Rose noticed her being very quiet. She thought that she might be missing her family at home. Rose asked Evelyn while walking to the restaurant, "Are you okay?"

"Of course," said Evelyn in a chirpy voice. "Why you ask?"

Rose chuckled. "Because you haven't said two words and we have been out for several hours now."

"I'm okay, Rose. Don't worry about me. I'm enjoying the Caribbean vibe. I'm taking in all the sights, the people and the food. It's so laid back here. I'm trying to picture you and Frank here. You two seem to be so busy most of the time"

Rose laughs "I know, but believe me, Frank loves this place. He's most relaxed here, and I love it, too. That's why the wedding's here."

"Wonderful," Evelyn said.

Chapter 25

Rose's Wedding Day Has Finally Arrived

ROSE STARTED HER DAY WITH a cup of coffee, sitting on her villa deck, looking out toward a gorgeous sunrise and the calm ocean water that seemed to speak to her in every flap of a wave. She felt a sense of peace and tranquility. Rose was in deep thought. I want to remember this moment. So, Rose took out her iPhone and recorded the moment of tranquility. She pointed her phone toward the ocean, and just a few minutes into her recording, she saw a whale, far out into the ocean.

Struck with awe, Rose kept recording and yelled out, "O-M-G! Out of all the days in my life and going out whale watching, I finally see a whale, on my wedding day." And then she saw two whales, flying in and out of the water over and over, twirling in the air as if they were giving her a private show.

Rose continued to record the whales for anyone that would not believe her morning view. She got a kick out of when the whales squirted water from their blowholes as if they were making umbrellas. The show lasted for about three minutes, but Rose was very excited to have been given a private whale show. She named the two whales,

Rose's Story

Shimmer and Shine.

Rose got up and walked toward the villa's glass door entrance, but before entering, she looked back at the beautiful bridal setup. The canopy was two steps below the guest seating area, which was decked out with palm tree branches. White and pink accented daffodils flowers were placed neatly around the arch. The fairy dust lights were placed throughout the canopy. When they were turned on, they would give the scene a romantic beach feel.

The guest seating area was set in two rows, which would be enough seating for the invited guests. It also had the same white daffodils flowers draped on the seating headrest.

The guests would not miss seeing the bride and groom reciting their vows under the beautiful sets of soft lighting that twinkled against a starry night sky. The ocean was their canvas along with an ocean breeze and softly crashing waves.

Rose wanted the evening to be a romantic affair. She hoped that they would enjoy the laid-back atmosphere.

The food would be set up on the beach under an oversized white linen tent. She thought to rope the side walls open to view the moonlit sky, shining above the ocean. If not, the tent would have windows for continuous views of the night sky.

With so much excitement, Rose was happy that this day had finally arrived. It was still very early in the morning. Chef Brew would be arriving around one o'clock in the afternoon to get the food started. DJ Spin and his crew needed to setup his DJ booth and dance floor.

Big Eaze had a section of the beach cut off from beachgoers, where the Barbados beach patrol officers would be setting up their Jeeps to block off any uninvited guests.

Rose, again, took in the moment and snapped more pictures. She walked into the villa, where she now saw Evelyn making spinach omelets and adding colorful bell peppers, hash browns, and freshly squeezed orange juice. Evelyn asked Rose if she would like some breakfast. Both women sat and ate while chatting about what the day would be like.

Evelyn asked Rose, "Are you nervous?"

"No, I'm not. This is one of our favorite areas to visit, so I'm pretty much comfortable with the setting. I'm hoping to get through my vows a lot smoother than the last time."

Rose and Evelyn laughed at how Rose had handled her practice run a couple of weeks ago. She'd found herself stumbling and mixing up her vows at the rehearsal dinner.

Evelyn wanted to give Rose a little encouragement, so she said, "Take a deep breath and breathe out slowly. Don't rush through it. Take your time. Savor the moment, and you'll do just fine."

"Thanks, Evelyn. You are a real friend. I appreciate your encouraging words. I'll try it."

Both women looked at each other, smiling with gratitude at each other.

Scarlet came into the kitchen to fix herself some breakfast. She sat next to Rose and said that she would like to invite Tide to the wedding reception.

"Oh, okay. I see you hanging with that guy a lot," Rose said.

"No, you don't. You're barely here when he drops me off," said Scarlet. "He's a lot of fun and a very interesting guy."

"Well, I know now." Rose laughed. "Be safe. If this was to go further, how would you date? Most of the time, you're across seas,

Rose's Story

prompting your lip fashion."

"I don't know, but we'll figure that out together," Scarlet said. "Right now, we're just getting to know each other. We both have demanding jobs and…"

Rose interrupted her, "Yup, and his job is all year 'round. There are no winter breaks here in Barbados."

"Yeah, yeah," said Scarlet. "Well, the time is going by fast. Just a few more hours and you will be a married woman." Scarlet looked for a response from Rose.

Rose responded by saying, "I know, but honestly we have lived like a married couple for the past seven years. It's time to do the darn thing and live an honest life. We have a lot of things together." She stopped herself. And then she said, "Yeah, it's time, and he's ready."

"Are you nervous?" asked Scarlet.

"Not at all," said Rose. "I'm ready to get it over with. I have mentioned to him that I need my me time back. I'm exhausted with all the running here and there. There's going to be some changes soon. So, with that said…" Rose looked at all three women (Ruby and Bubbles had entered the kitchen for some breakfast). "I would like to have a women's retreat on the island of Fiji." Rose smiled at them.

No one said anything.

"Well, we all don't have to speak at once," said Rose.

Ruby said, "Let's just get this wedding out the way, and then, when you come back from your honeymoon, we can talk about it. By the way, where are you going on your honeymoon?"

"Funny. We haven't talk about it. I'm not sure," said Rose. "Frank has been so busy with opening up the restaurant in Santa Monica, we have not talked about going away."

"I'm sure you two will be going somewhere, maybe to your very own private island," said Ruby.

"And that would be nice, as long as he doesn't go to work." Rose laughed.

Chapter 26

A Romantic Beach Wedding

Rose and Big Eaze married on Crane Beach in Barbados. It was five o'clock in the afternoon, and Rose was dressed in her custom-made wedding dress, designed by her eleven-year-old granddaughter Bubbles, aka Me'chelle. Her hair stylist pinned her hair up in a bun, adding precious pearls flown in from Athens, Greece. Rose requested to wear very little to no makeup. She'd chosen a French manicure for her hands and feet, which went well with her beach sandals which were also laced with pearls and looked very much like the pearls in her hair.

They all gathered together and admired each other. The Divas and Bubbles looked spectacular in their Caribbean turquoise sea gowns, which had all been custom-made and fit them to a T. They had tried on the dresses at the beginning of the week and had watched what they ate and exercised to keep at their current weight. If not, Carlotta was on standby to help the women fit into those beautiful gowns.

They could hear the music playing and guests laughing and talking among themselves.

Evelyn came in with updates that all the guests had arrived and that Big Eaze's groomsmen had also finally arrived and that they were now talking to the priest. She said that there was a light breeze coming off the ocean, but overall, it was a beautiful day.

Scarlet stood up and said that it was time for them to leave.

As they prepared to get in position near the canopy, waiting for the bride. Ruby and Bubbles followed suit.

"We'll see you in about thirty minutes and don't be late." Ruby laughed.

Suddenly, Rose felt nervous, but she took Evelyn's advice to try to calm her nerves. She breathed in and breathed out slowly. With that exercise, she felt a sense of peace.

Rose and Evelyn sat quietly until it was time to leave. Twenty-five minutes went by fast, Rose had five minutes left as Rose Crystal.

She heard her cue, a song that she and Big Eaze had picked out. She would walk into his arms and vow to be Mrs. Rose Crystal Zaiders.

The sunset above the ocean water was a beautiful fiery red with orange rays of light. It had never disappointed the Barbadian residents, and now it would not disappoint Rose and Big Eaze on their wedding day.

The lights on the deck and canopy came on, which peered through a man-made misty fog as Rose walked the villa deck to "You and I" by KeKe Wyatt and Avant. She took Big Eaze's hand, and they danced and serenaded each other. The guests stood and cheered them, applauding them on such a beautiful song selection.

Once the song was over, they stood in front of the priest, ready to recite their vows. Big Eaze kept smiling at Rose. It took so much for

Rose's Story

him not to hug her, but he whispered to her, "You look like a delicate rose petal."

Rose winked and blew Big Eaze a kiss.

There was always someone that cried at weddings, but from the view, everyone was shedding a tear because everyone's hearts were filled with joy for Rose and Big Eaze as they recited their vows to each other. Rose nailed it by taking her time, which gave a heartfelt meaning to words. After they had both recited their vows, the priest pronounced them husband and wife.

The guests were given a confetti of flowers, and once the bride and groom turned around to face all their guests, a sea of flowers was tossed into the air, going against a breeze, floating above the bride and groom and all the guests.

All of this was being recorded from the villa deck camera.

Cheers and congrats were yelled out, and there were a lot of laughter, and everyone trying to speak at once … "We're so happy for you and Frank! Mr. & Mrs. Zaiders! Happy wife! Happy life!" All the guests had wished them well.

The wedding was so beautiful.

The guests were guided to the beach area, which was just a few steps from the villa, for food and drinks and, of course, partying Rose and Big Eaze-style all throughout the night.

Rose and Big Eaze shared their first dance as husband and wife. Big Eaze had chosen "Lady" by the Whispers, knowing that it was one of Rose's favorite group and one of their favorite song.

After playing the bride and groom's first song, DJ Spinn did his best with the musical selections. He played island music and reggae, which included a lot of the Marley family's music.

DJ Spinn sang along while he played "Is this Love?" by Bob Marley. He patted his chest and sang *"that I'm feeling"* all while looking toward Ruby.

He'd also hired a local Barbadian band to mix in with the current music he played. They played those special steel drums that Rose had requested. It was a great mix of music that DJ Spinn played, and the band stayed in tune with DJ Spinn.

Rose really enjoyed the steel drums and the congas as she swayed back and forth to much of the music. "You would think that she was an island girl," Evelyn said with a laugh.

They partied well into the a.m.. Rose now feeling a bit tired, wanted to call it a night.

She pulled the Divas aside and told to them, "Please have the staff clean the area. Have the chairs folded and the tables taken down. The rental company will be picking the tent up at about ten o'clock in the morning."

"Mom, we got this," said Ruby.

"Must we remind you again that we are event coordinators?" Scarlet asked.

The Divas did a two snap and swung their heads back, giving much attitude. Rose just looked at them with a blank stare. The Divas, then, hugged her and kissed her on the cheek.

"We love you, lady. Now go be with your husband," Ruby said with a laugh.

"I love you, too. You're my precious Jewels. Thanks for handling all of the wedding. I couldn't have done all of this without you girls and Bubbles. Where is she anyway? If not for the wedding, I would have barely seen her at all these past two weeks."

Rose's Story

"Well, she's been with Chef Brew and his family most of the two weeks," Ruby said.

"Oh, she's excited that she's able to do kids things again." Rose laughed.

Rose walked toward Big Eaze and mentioned to him that she was ready to leave but first wanted to thank the guests.

Big Eaze got the guests' attention. Then, he and Rose thanked them for joining them on their special day and wishing them well. Rose blew kisses and gave out hugs as she and Big Eaze eased their way out of the reception. Big Eaze held his bride close to him.

Chapter 27

Nights like This

Rose and Big Eaze sat alone on their villa deck, looking out onto the moonlit ocean waters. Rose laid her head on Big Eaze's shoulder and held onto his arm. She told Big Eaze that she was very happy that this day had finally arrived.

Then, Big Eaze said, "I told you that everything would go well, you just have to believe and go with the flow. Don't overexert yourself, getting all work up, stressing yourself out. You have a staff that loves you and has been by our side for years." Big Eaze was talking about Evelyn. "They know what to do at all times. Trust them, Rose." He planted a kiss her on her forehead.

Big Eaze pulled a small piece of paper out of his pants pocket and said, "Oh, what is this?" He was holding the small piece of paper in the air. He then gave that small piece of paper to Rose.

Rose saw her name in bolded, red glitter letters. She unfolded the neatly folded piece of paper. Then, she looked up at Big Eaze and laughed and said, "Really," and read out loud what was written on the paper:

"To my beautiful, lovely, and wonderful wife, Rose, we've been together well over fifteen years. Sorry it took so long to get to this special day, with us now becoming one. I've always been about work, building a brand from the ground up. Now that I have you by my-side every day, I am now a complete man, and I thank you for standing by my side at countless meetings, luncheons, and dinner parties and, most of all, for helping to manage our enterprises. After all of this, we are ready to …

Then, she slowly read, "Yacht the Mediterranean Sea on your brand new one hundred sixty-five feet superyacht called "**Rose**."

Rose could not believe what she had read, so she read it again. She now understood why he hadn't mentioned a honeymoon.

Rose wrapped her arms around Big Eaze's neck and gave him a big hug and thanked him for the wonder gift. While hugging him, Rose was a bit curious and thought about this proposal, Will we be conducting business on the yacht or wherever we're stationed? So, Rose asked, "No meetings?"

Big Eaze laughed. "Of course not. This is for us to enjoy. We will conduct business when we return in six months."

Rose's mouth dropped. "What? How can you be away that long without working?"

"Let me handle that area," said Big Eaze. "We deserve some time alone. Once we return to the states, we'll prepare for our trip".

"Like how soon can we leave for this specular journey on the open sea?" asked Rose.

"Anytime you like. I don't want to rush you. I want you to be ready and in the right state of mind. I want this to be adventurous, a bit exciting." As Rose looked at Big Eaze, he continued, "And of course, relaxing."

Rose giggled. "O-M-G! Frank, this is so over the top. I'm so excited. I'll get the staff prepared to be off for a few months, and we'll go from there." She looked into Big Eaze's eyes and said, "Thank you so much. We need this. I love you, Frank Zaiders."

"And I love you, Mrs. Rose Zaiders," Big Eaze said.

The End

Carla Cuffee residences in Pennsylvania with her two adult children and young grandchild.

When not writing her volume series on Rose's Story: Carla fills her day with her close connection, of family and friends. Her hobbies include reading, writing, and her version of art as … "♥'s It's me CC."

www.ingramcontent.com/pod-product-compliance
Lightning Source LLC
Chambersburg PA
CBHW070115080526
44586CB00013B/1299